Reflections Of A Royal Rose

I0834677

Dr. Claus

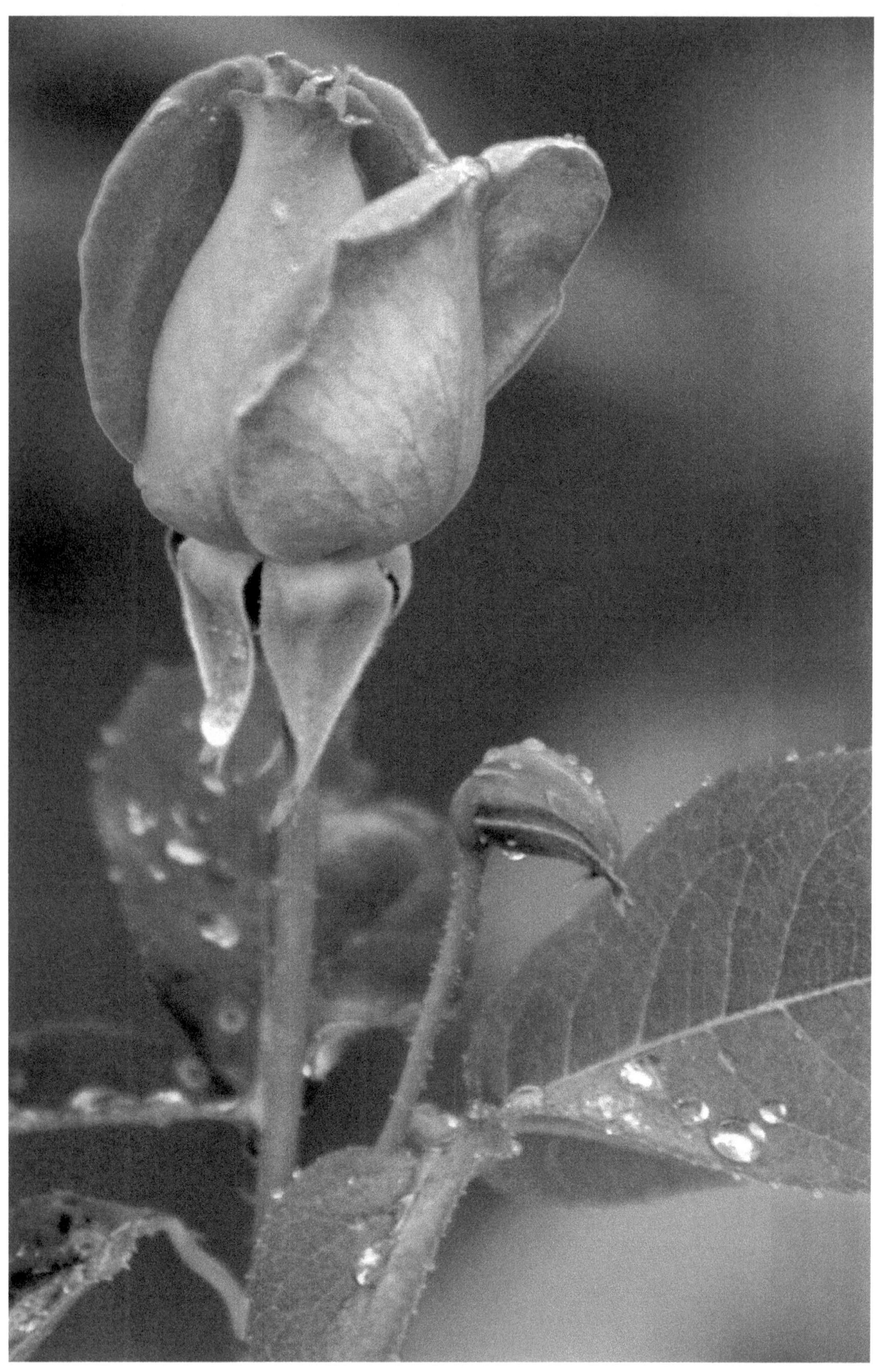

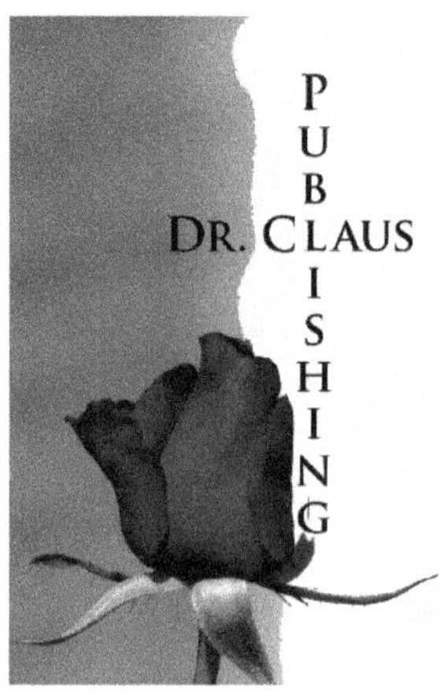

PUBLISHED BY DR. CLAUS PUBLISHING

First Edition
ISBN: 1-61497-060-2
ISBN-13: 978-1-61497-060-6
Library of Congress Control Number: 2015951065

DEDICATION

Virginia

CONTENTS

ACKNOWLEDGMENT

During the war, my heart of stone was taken from my chest.
In place of that stone, I received a heart of flesh.
My old heart was handed back to me and as I received this heart of stone,
my thumbprint was forever seared into this rock.
I carry this heart of stone with me wherever I may go.
On any given day when words of doubt rain down upon my soul,
I reach for a stone once embedded in my chest
and I place my thumb into the mark.

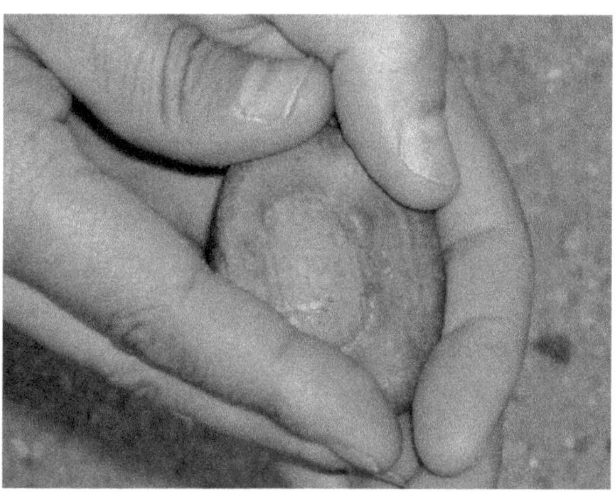

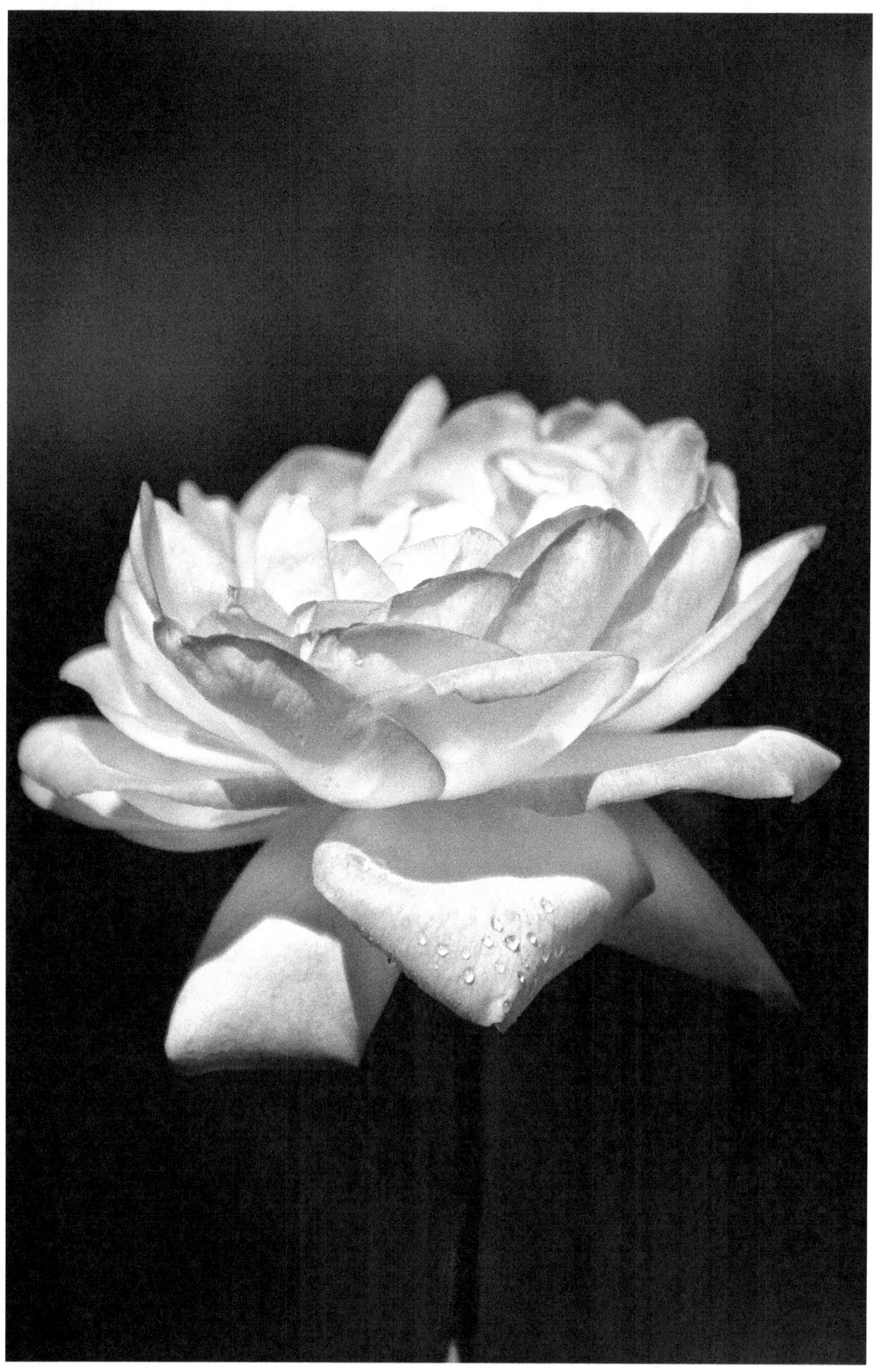

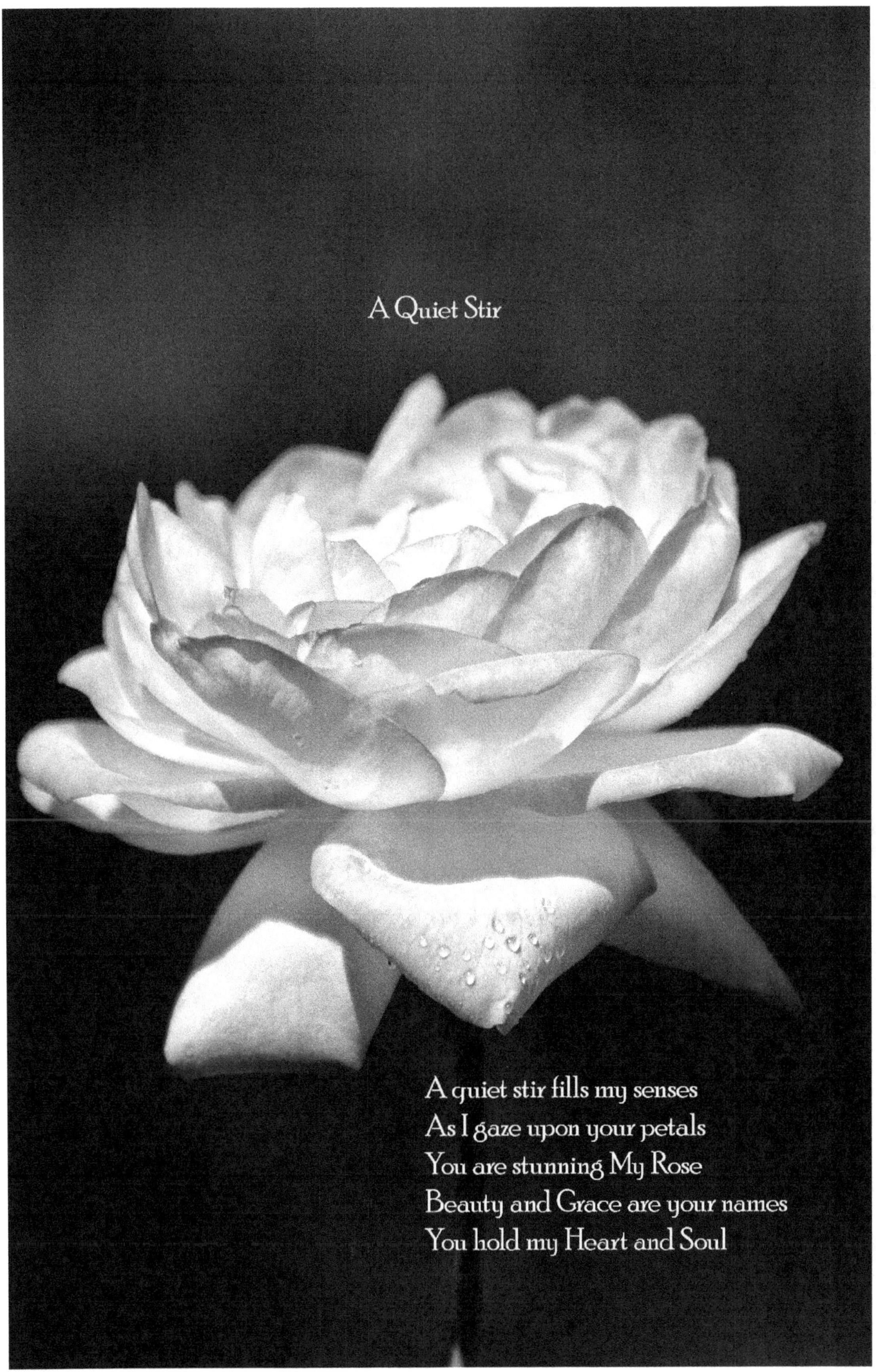
A Quiet Stir
A quiet stir fills my senses
As I gaze upon your petals
You are stunning My Rose
Beauty and Grace are your names
You hold my Heart and Soul

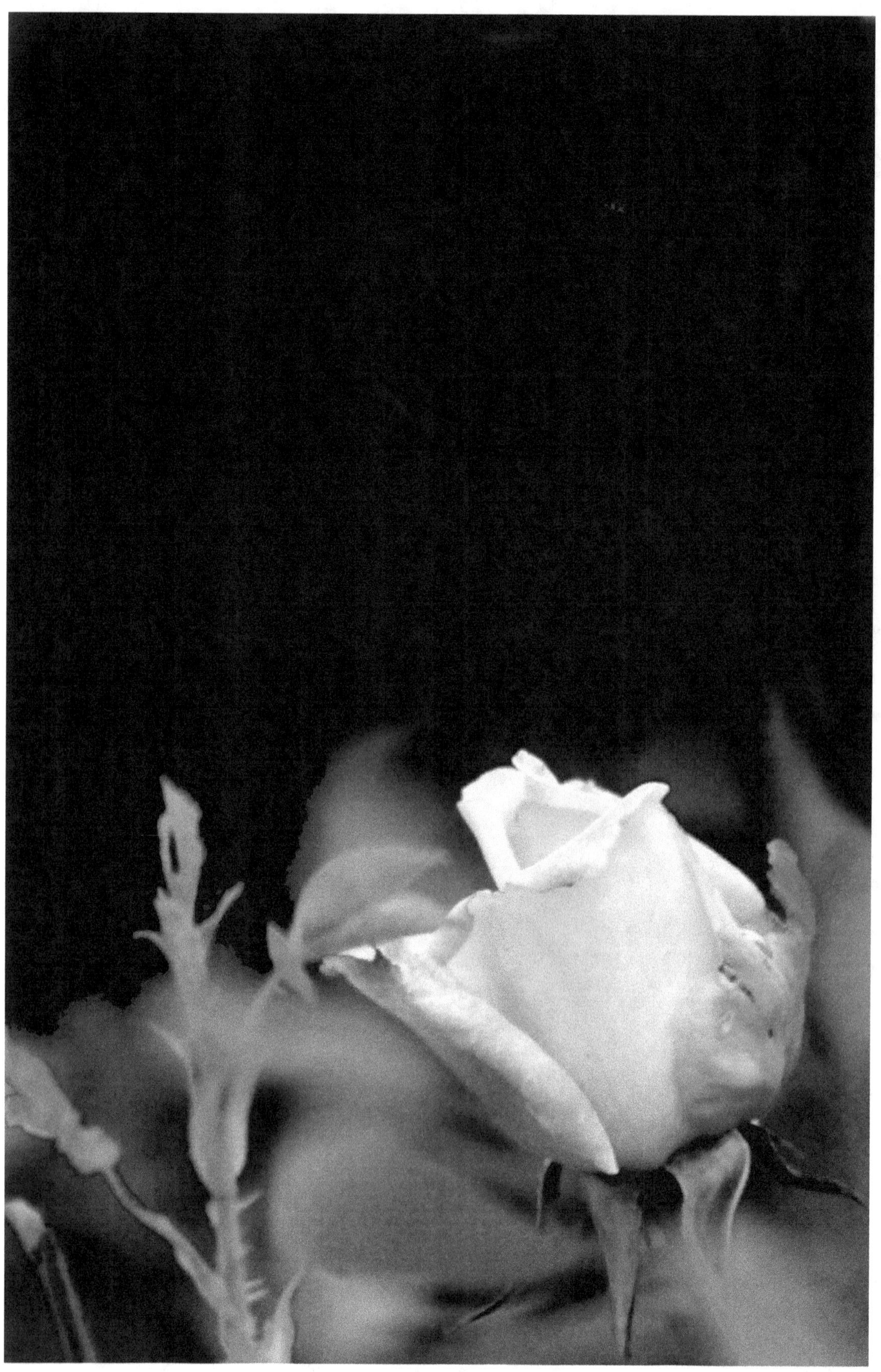

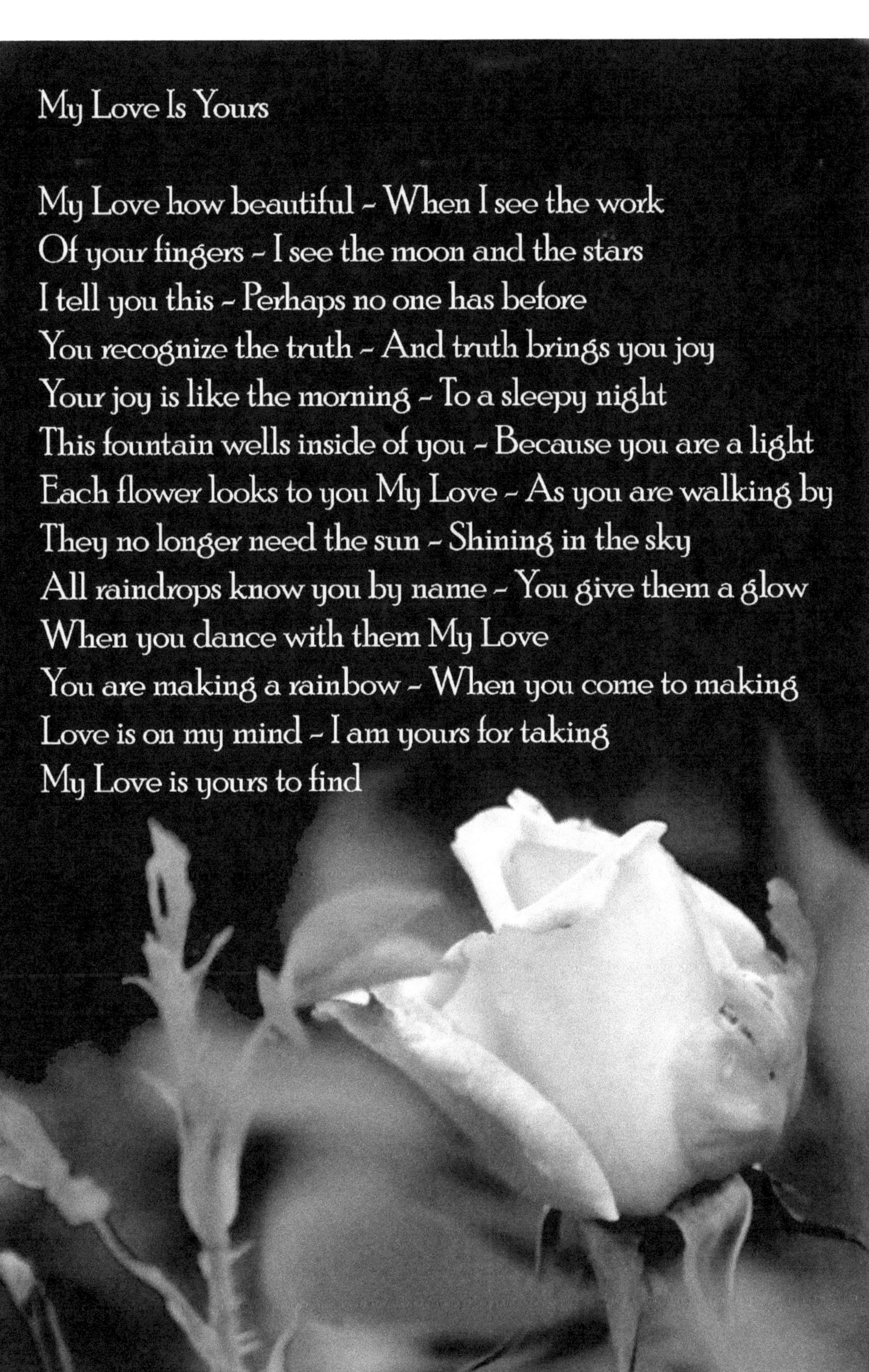

My Love Is Yours

My Love how beautiful - When I see the work
Of your fingers - I see the moon and the stars
I tell you this - Perhaps no one has before
You recognize the truth - And truth brings you joy
Your joy is like the morning - To a sleepy night
This fountain wells inside of you - Because you are a light
Each flower looks to you My Love - As you are walking by
They no longer need the sun - Shining in the sky
All raindrops know you by name - You give them a glow
When you dance with them My Love
You are making a rainbow - When you come to making
Love is on my mind - I am yours for taking
My Love is yours to find

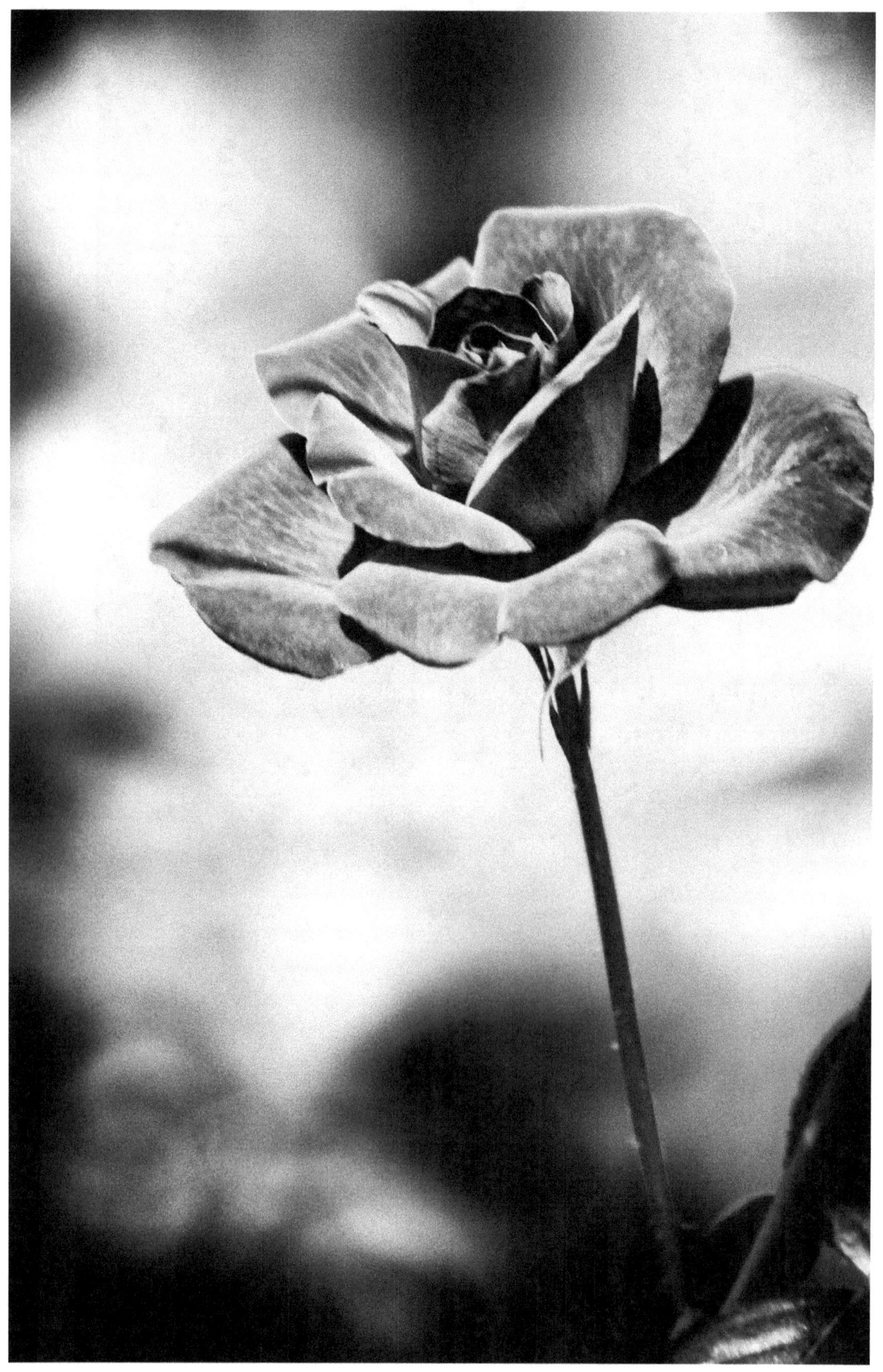

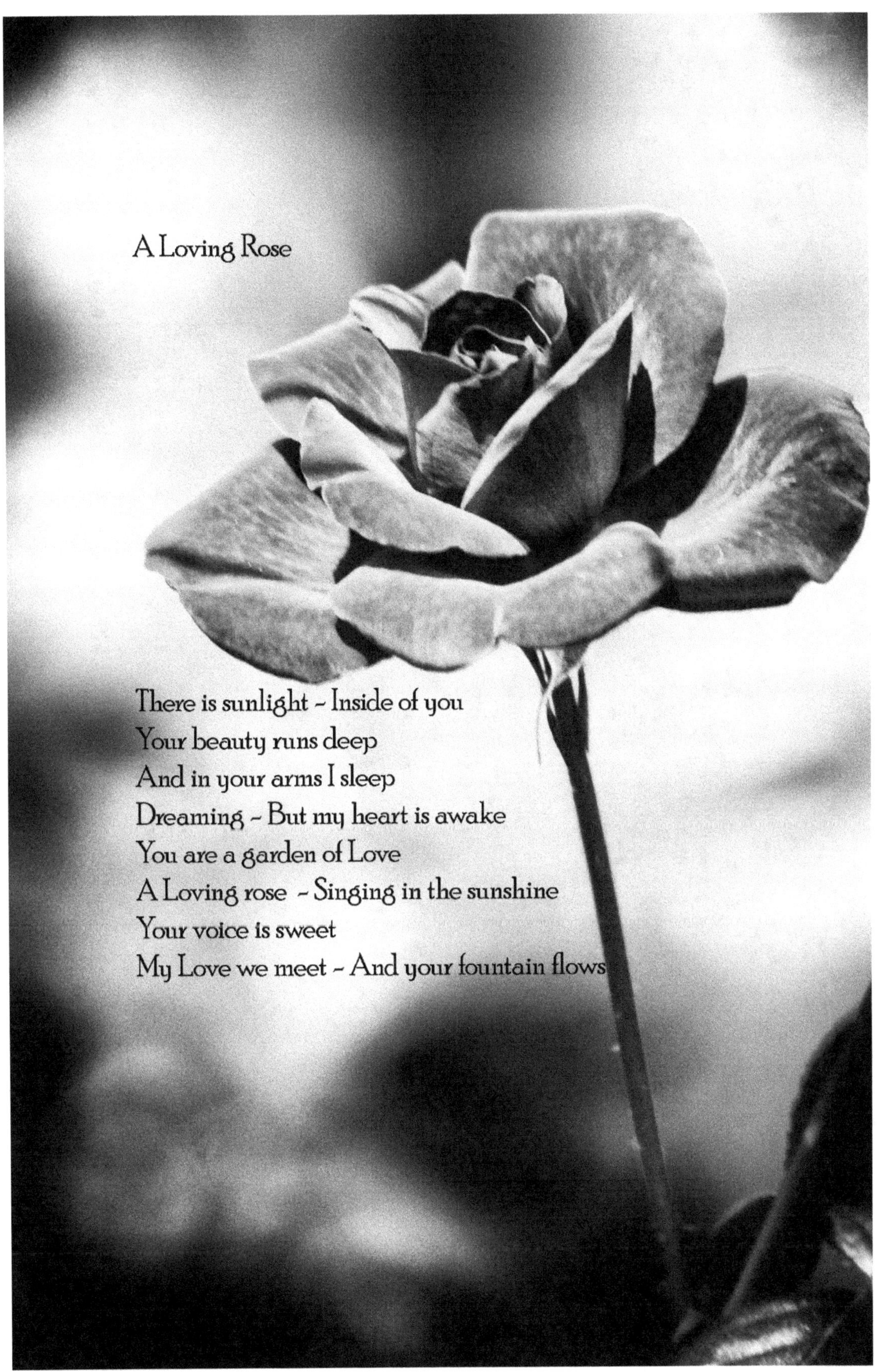

A Loving Rose

There is sunlight - Inside of you
Your beauty runs deep
And in your arms I sleep
Dreaming - But my heart is awake
You are a garden of Love
A Loving rose - Singing in the sunshine
Your voice is sweet
My Love we meet - And your fountain flows

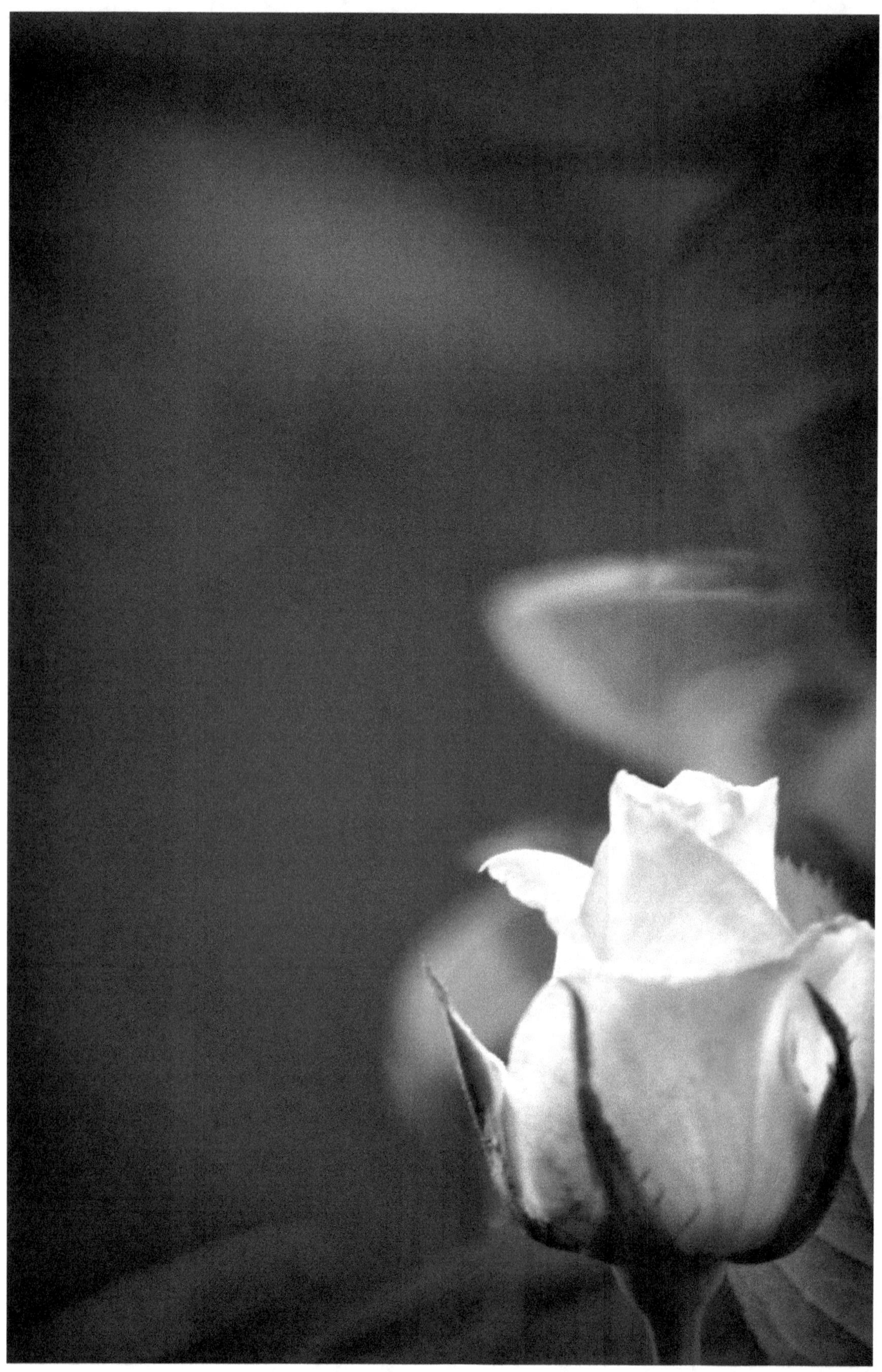

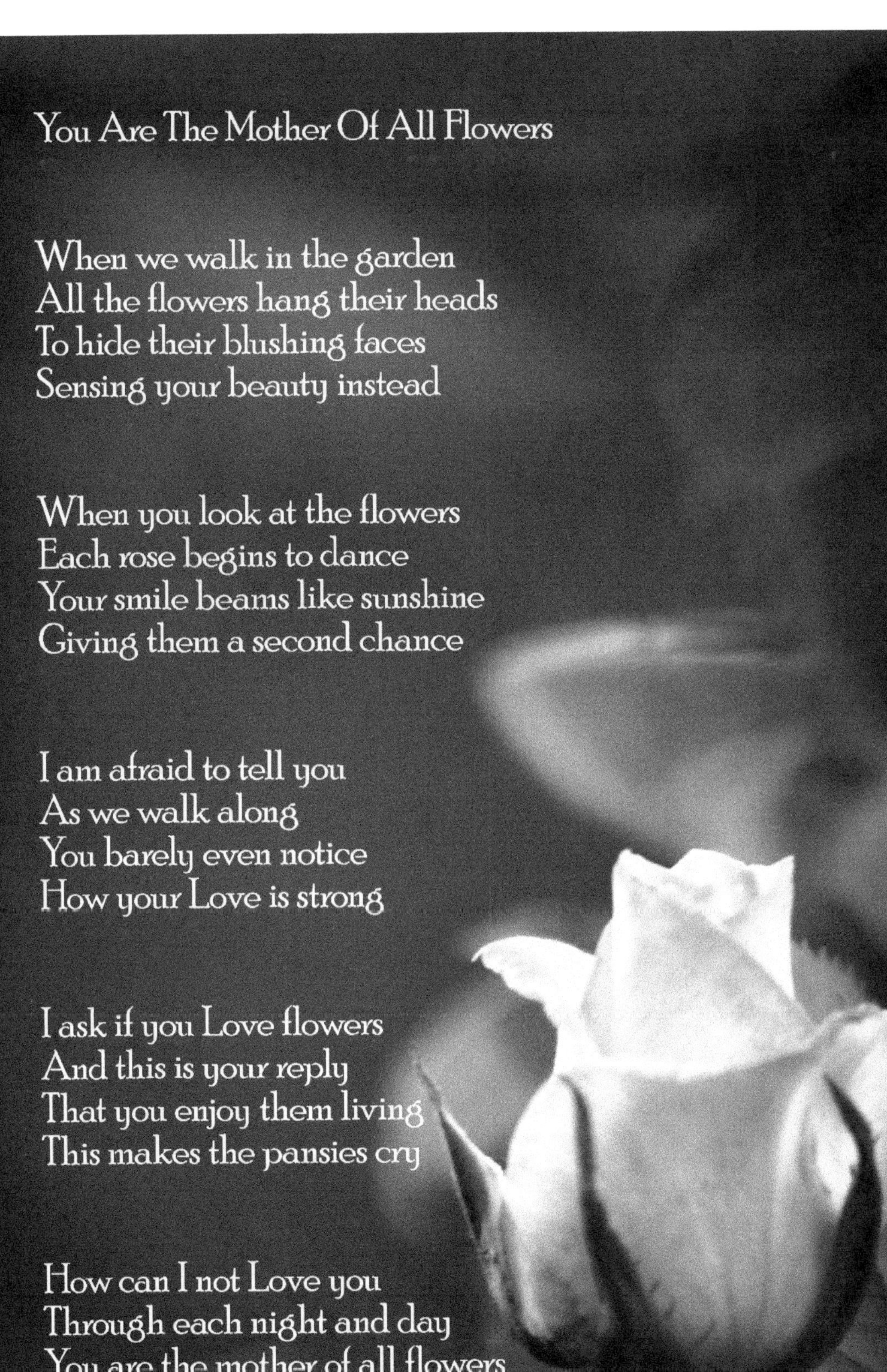

You Are The Mother Of All Flowers

When we walk in the garden
All the flowers hang their heads
To hide their blushing faces
Sensing your beauty instead

When you look at the flowers
Each rose begins to dance
Your smile beams like sunshine
Giving them a second chance

I am afraid to tell you
As we walk along
You barely even notice
How your Love is strong

I ask if you Love flowers
And this is your reply
That you enjoy them living
This makes the pansies cry

How can I not Love you
Through each night and day
You are the mother of all flowers
And they do as you say

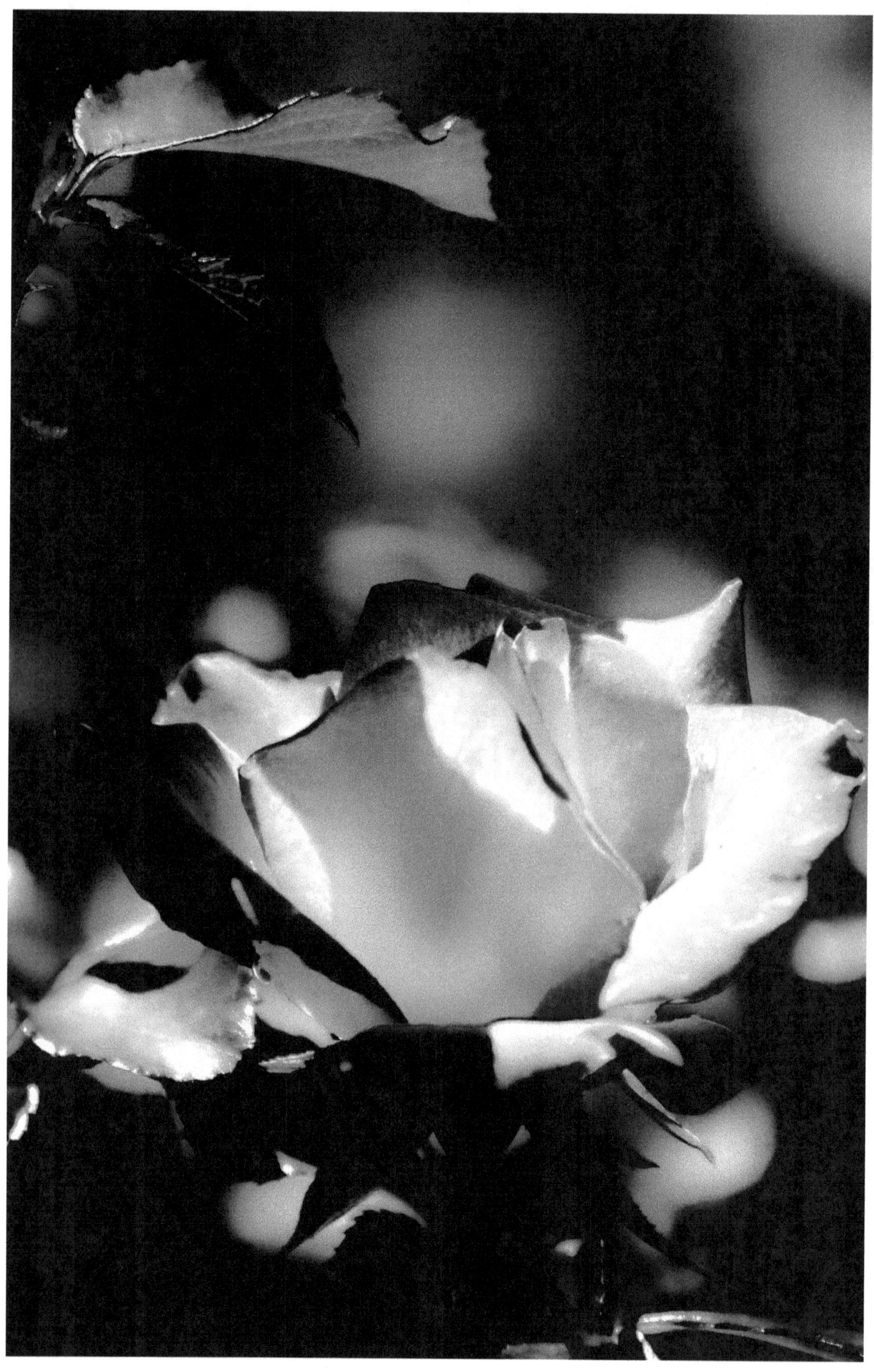

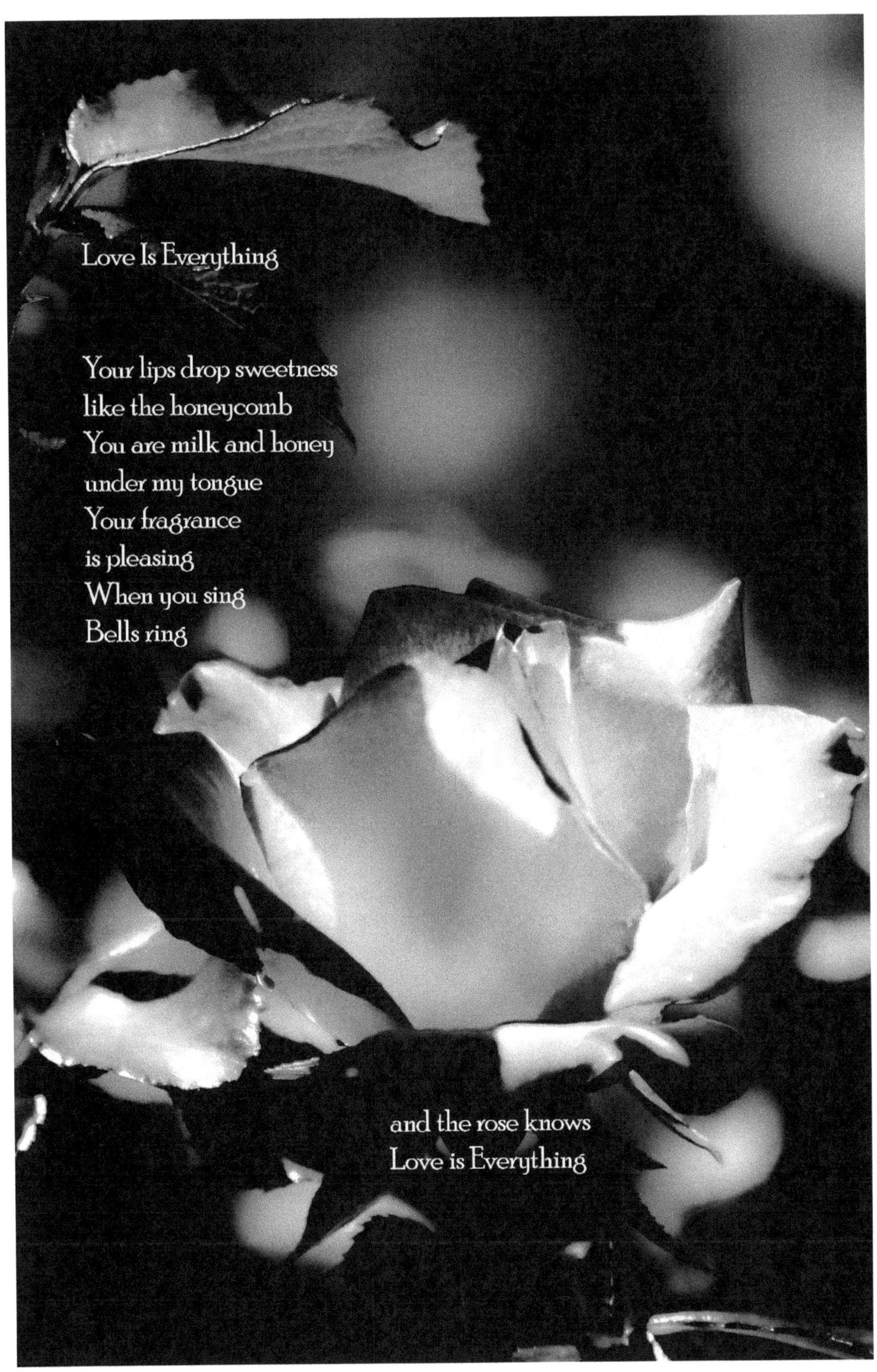
Love Is Everything
Your lips drop sweetness
like the honeycomb
You are milk and honey
under my tongue
Your fragrance
is pleasing
When you sing
Bells ring
and the rose knows
Love is Everything

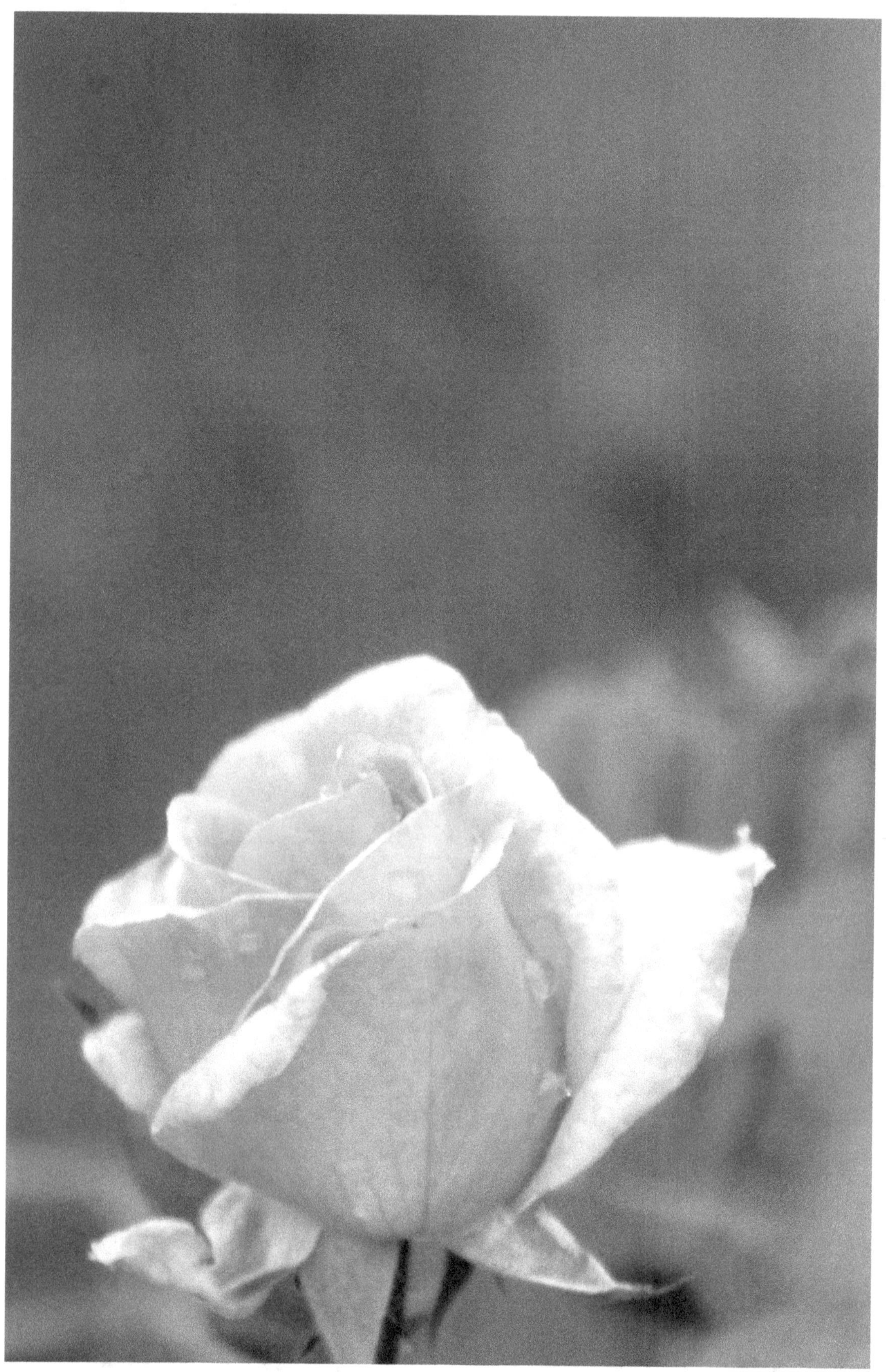

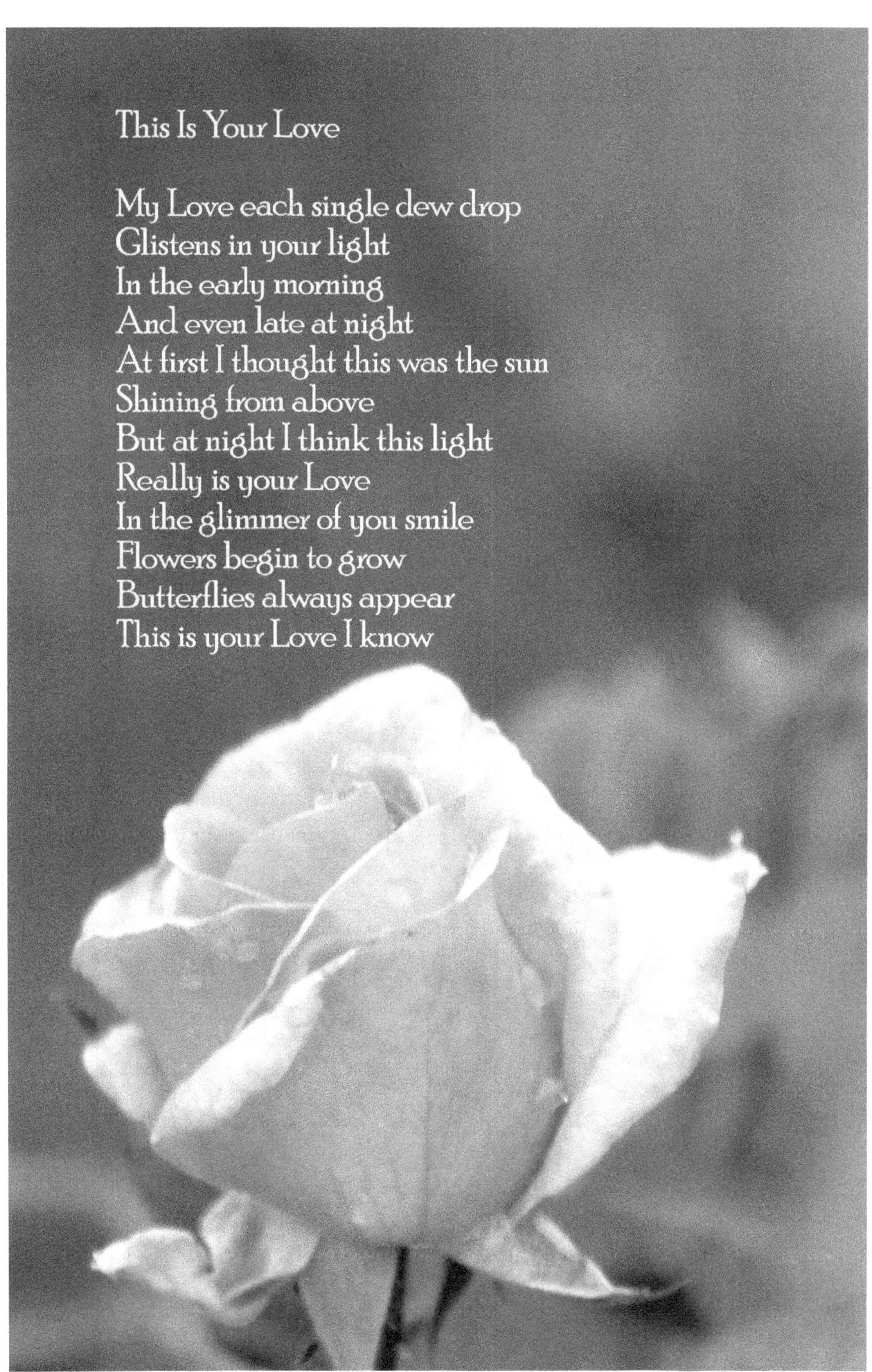

This Is Your Love

My Love each single dew drop
Glistens in your light
In the early morning
And even late at night
At first I thought this was the sun
Shining from above
But at night I think this light
Really is your Love
In the glimmer of you smile
Flowers begin to grow
Butterflies always appear
This is your Love I know

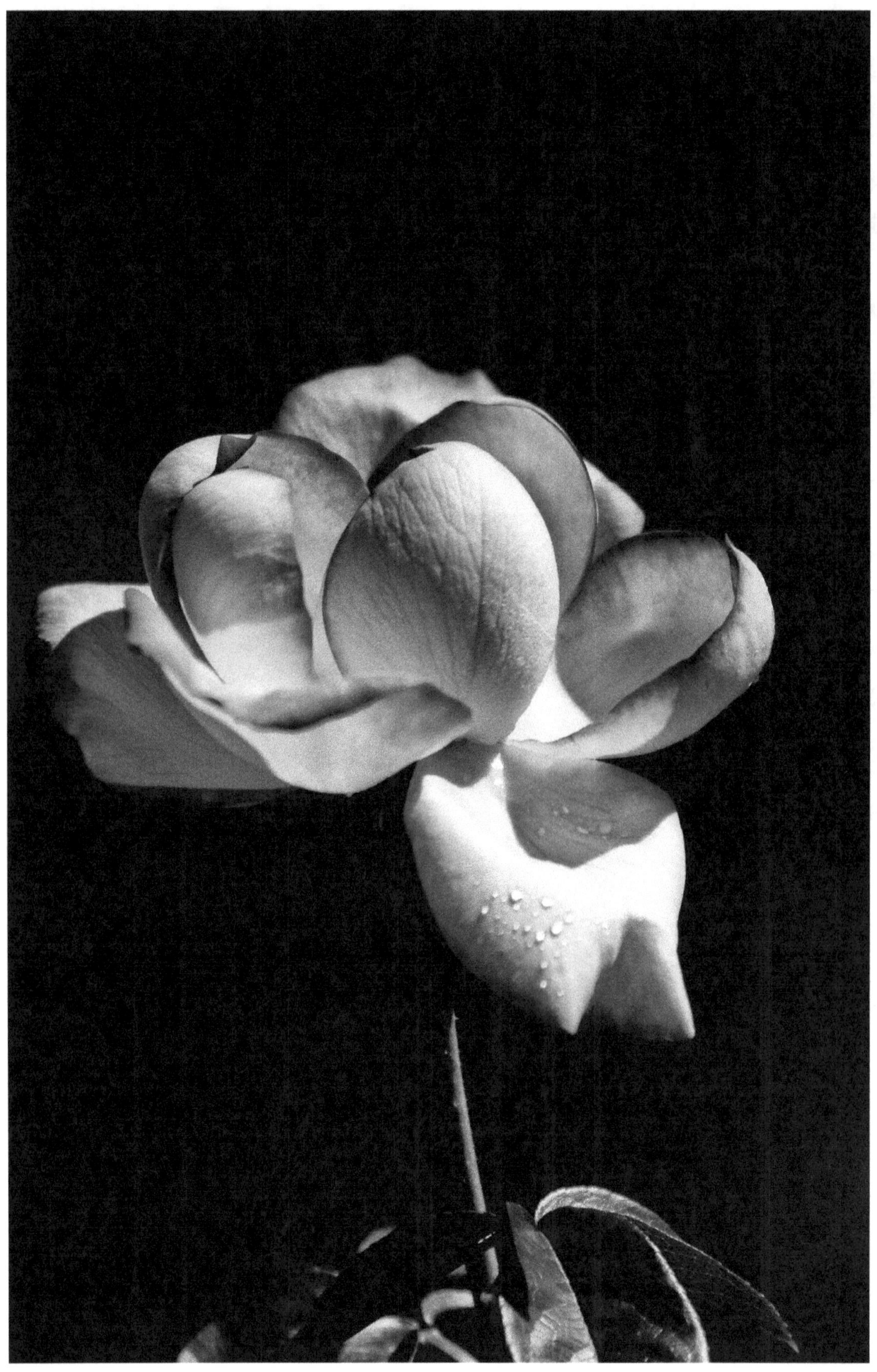

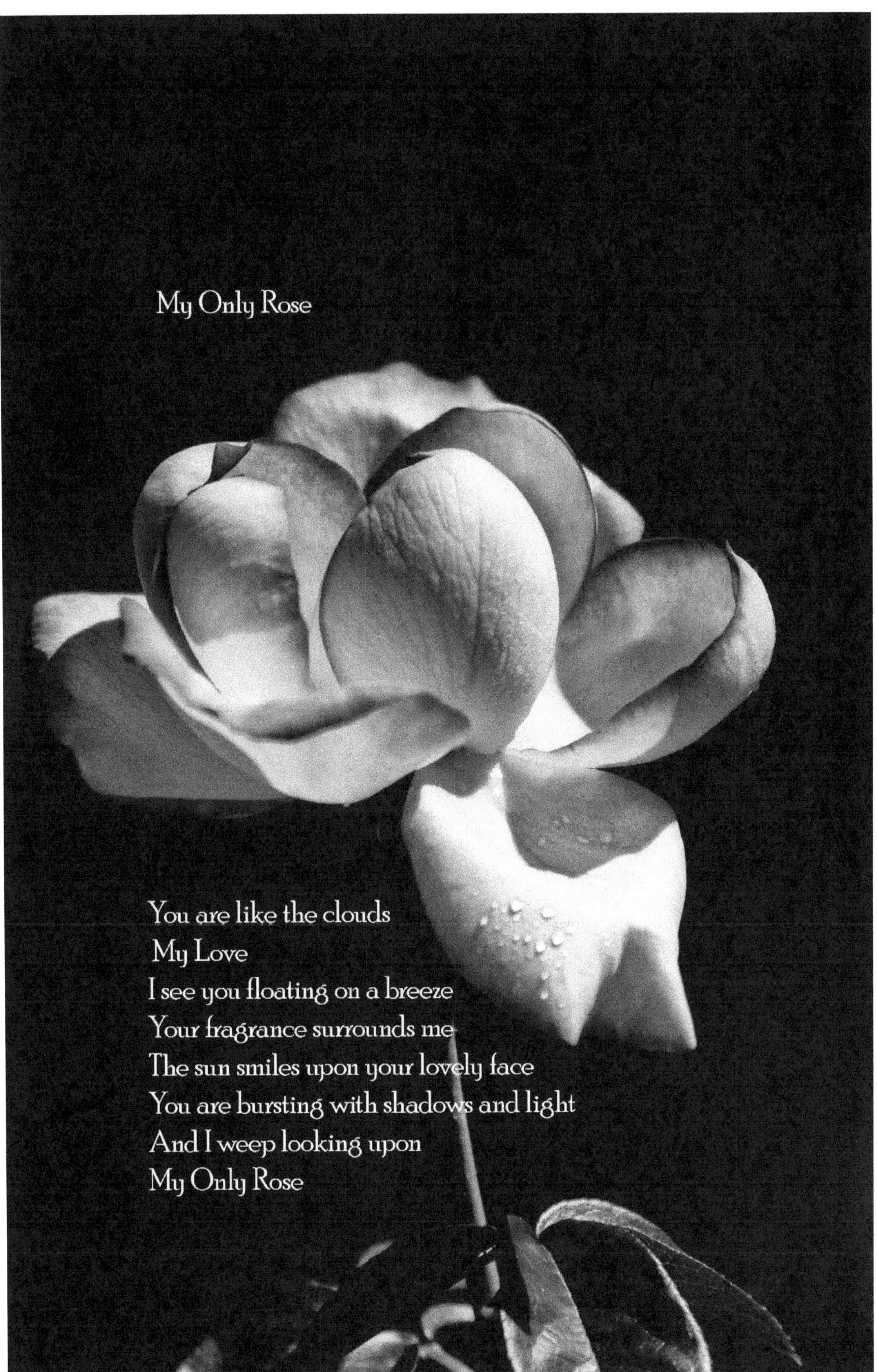

My Only Rose

You are like the clouds
My Love
I see you floating on a breeze
Your fragrance surrounds me
The sun smiles upon your lovely face
You are bursting with shadows and light
And I weep looking upon
My Only Rose

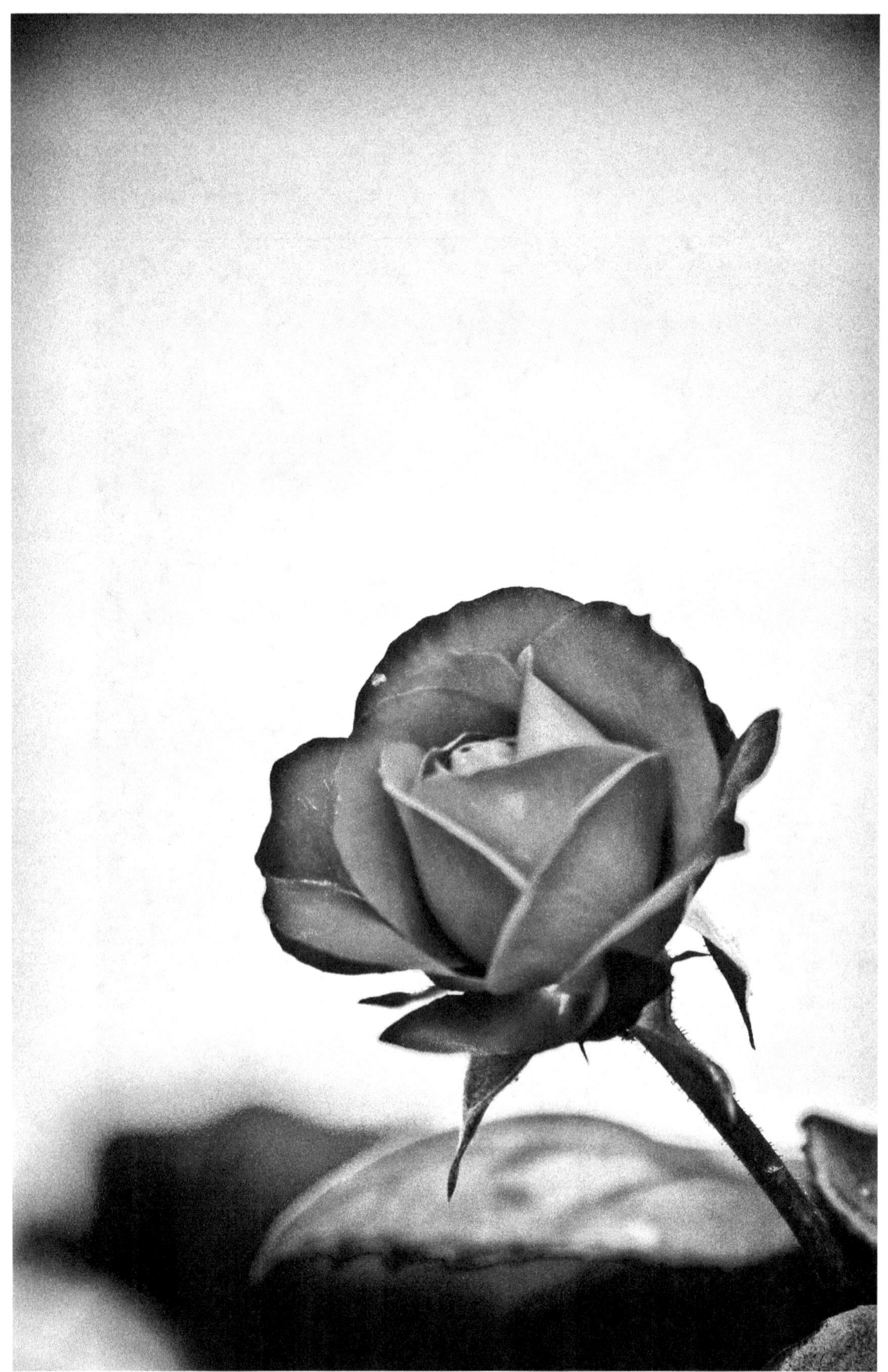

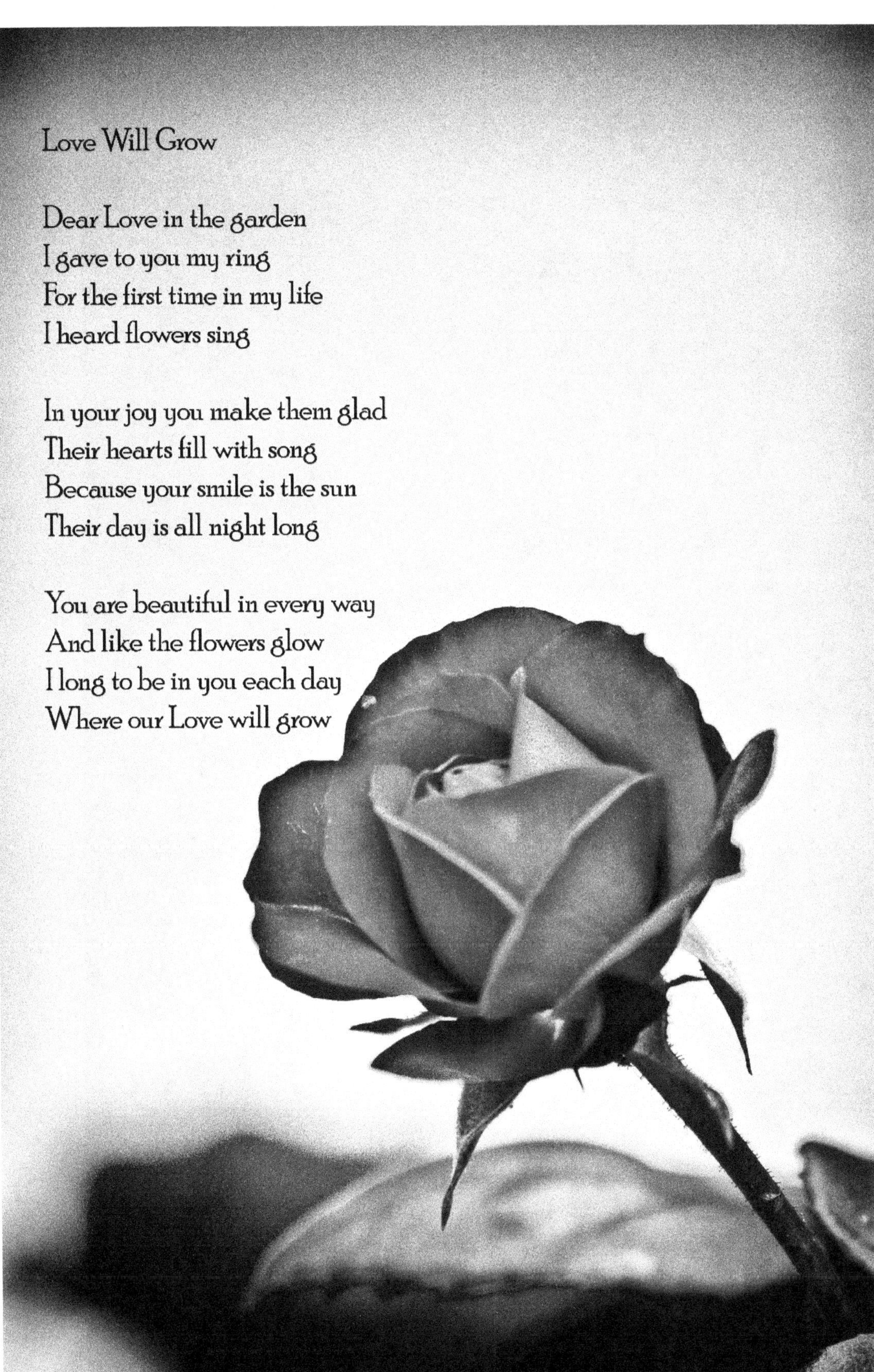

Love Will Grow

Dear Love in the garden
I gave to you my ring
For the first time in my life
I heard flowers sing

In your joy you make them glad
Their hearts fill with song
Because your smile is the sun
Their day is all night long

You are beautiful in every way
And like the flowers glow
I long to be in you each day
Where our Love will grow

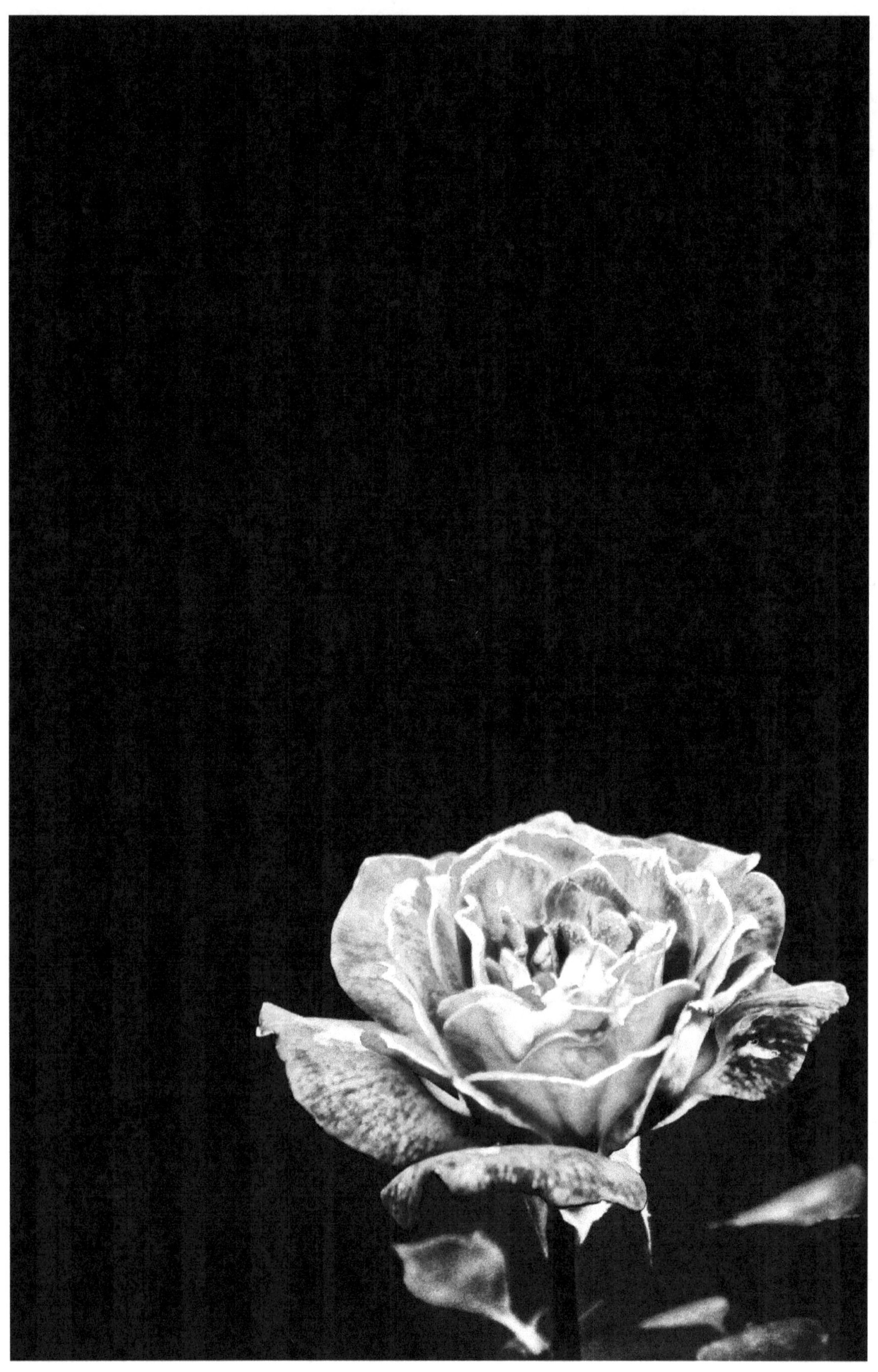

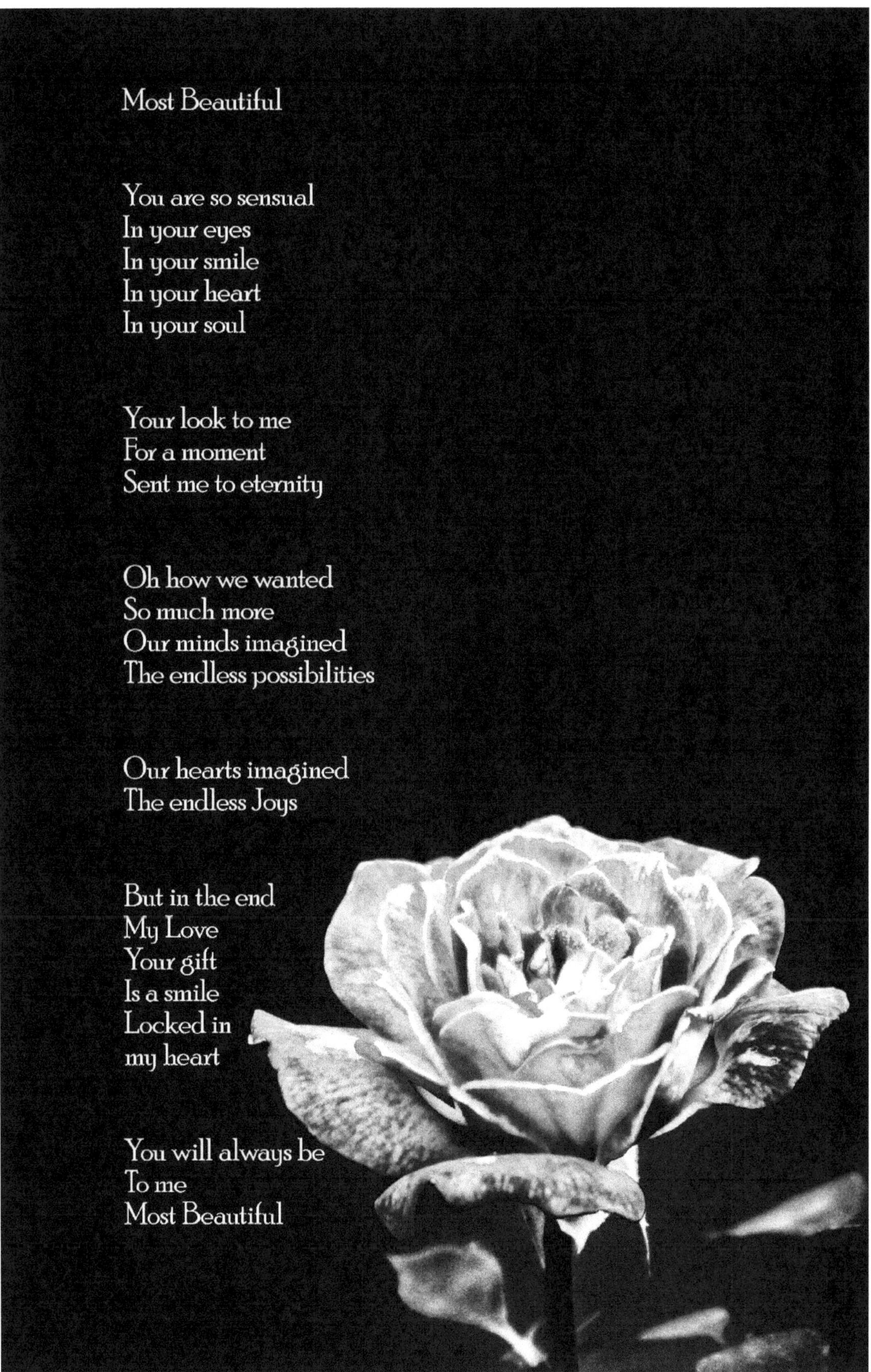

Most Beautiful

You are so sensual
In your eyes
In your smile
In your heart
In your soul

Your look to me
For a moment
Sent me to eternity

Oh how we wanted
So much more
Our minds imagined
The endless possibilities

Our hearts imagined
The endless Joys

But in the end
My Love
Your gift
Is a smile
Locked in
my heart

You will always be
To me
Most Beautiful

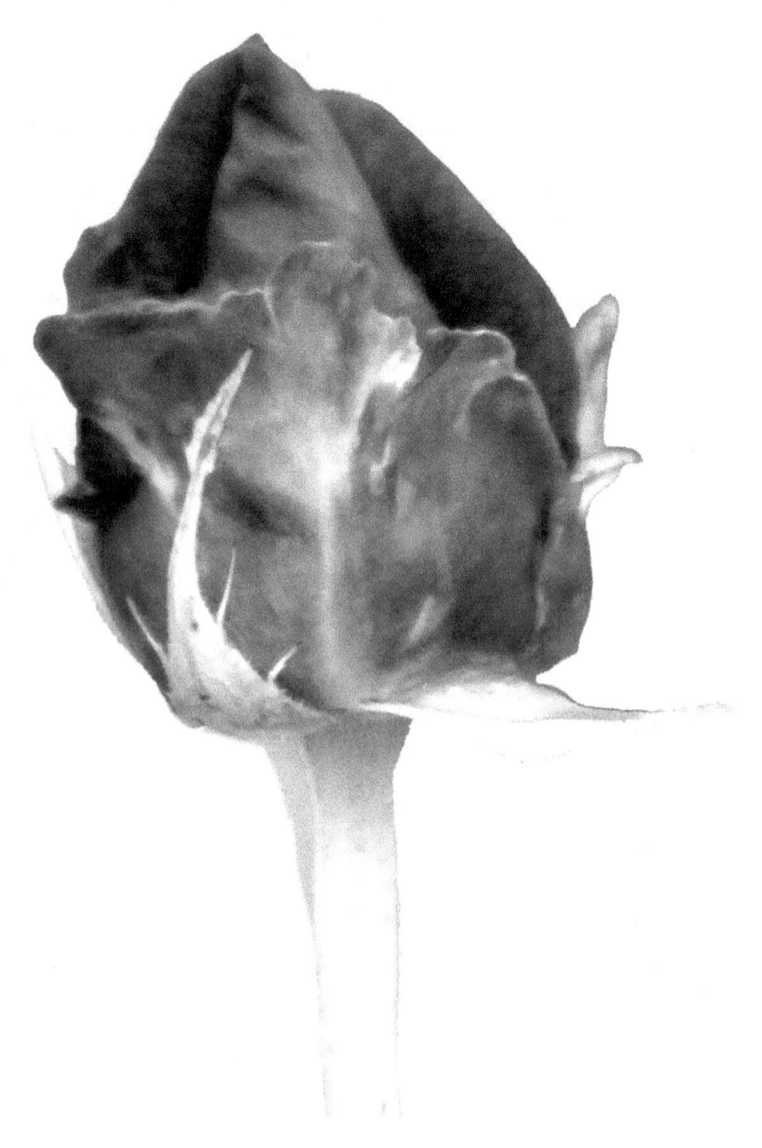

Kiss Me For Eternity

Good morning to the sun - To the moon and all the stars
Because every time I think of you - This is who you are

Your smile is the rising sun - Gently touching my face
Your eyes mirror the universe - Inner beauty is your grace

Your kiss stops my heart from beating - And set my soul free
Lovely lips so long and lush - Kiss me for eternity

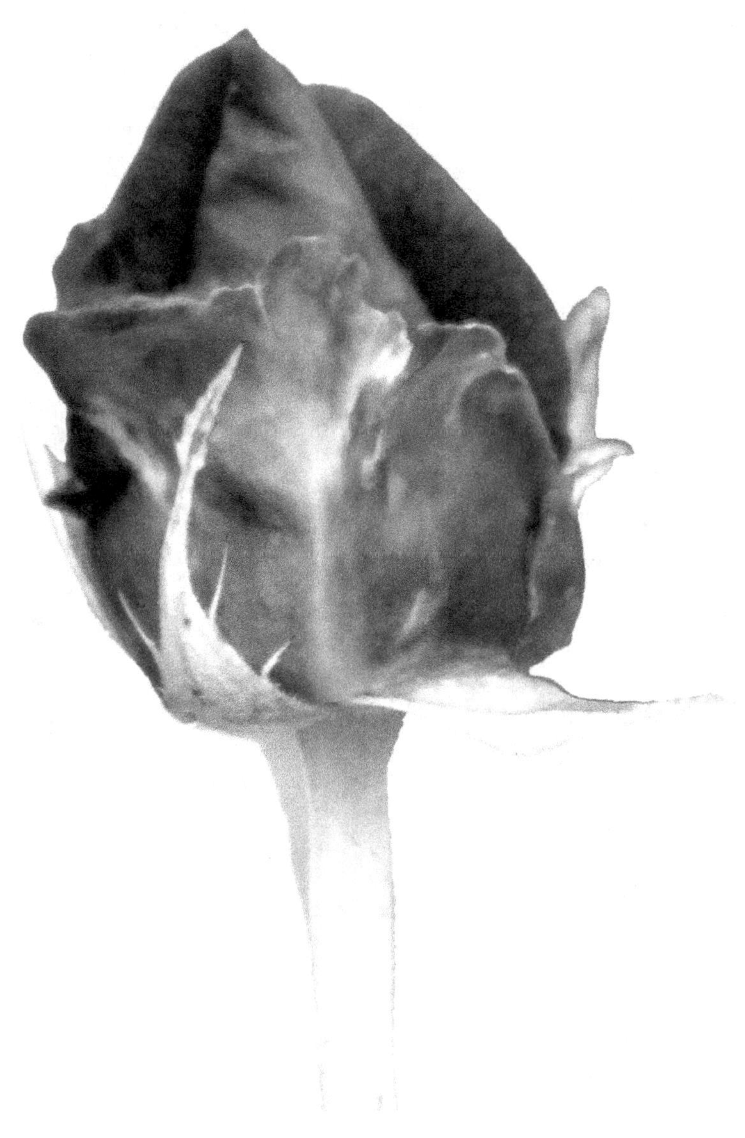

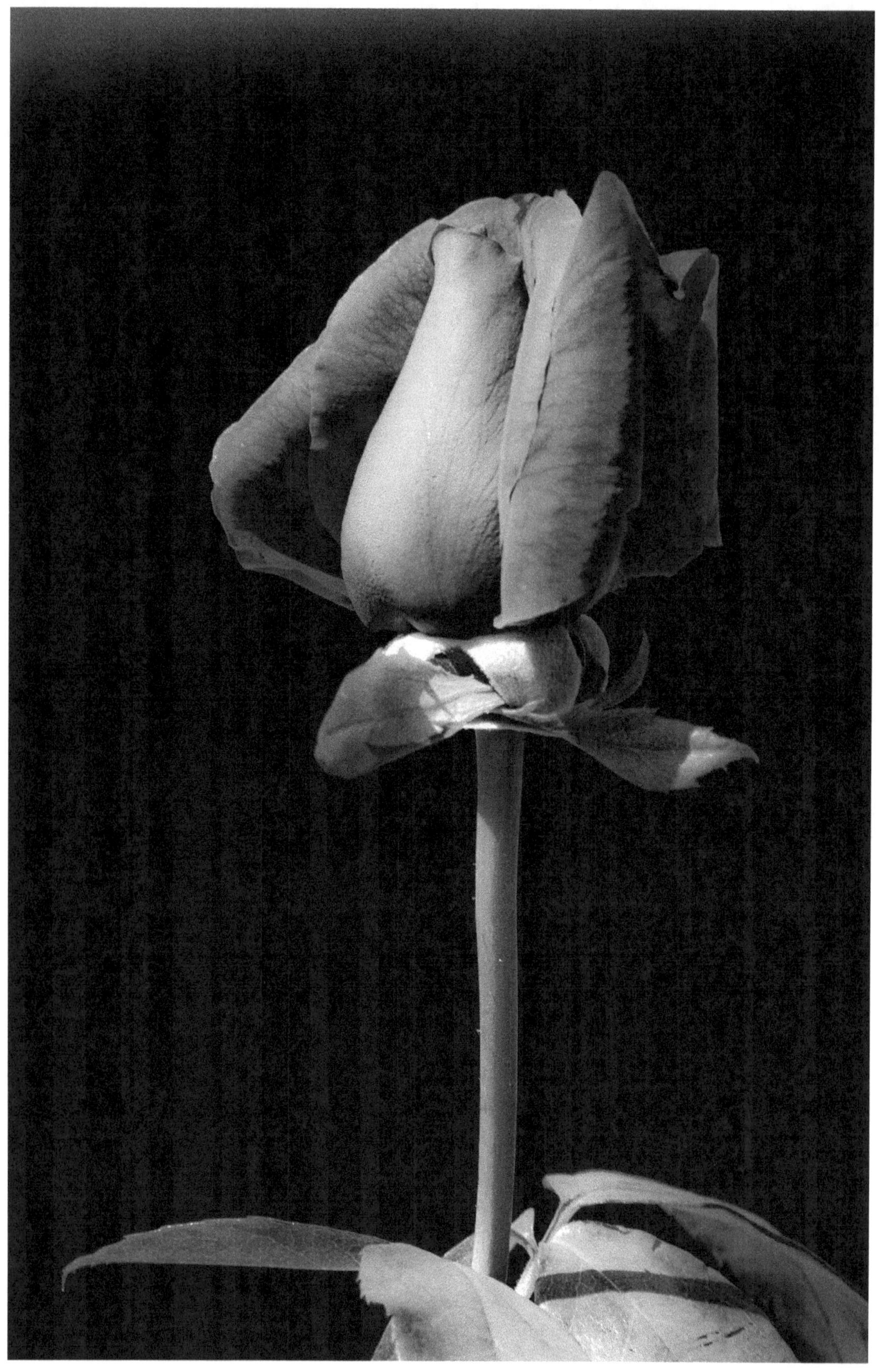

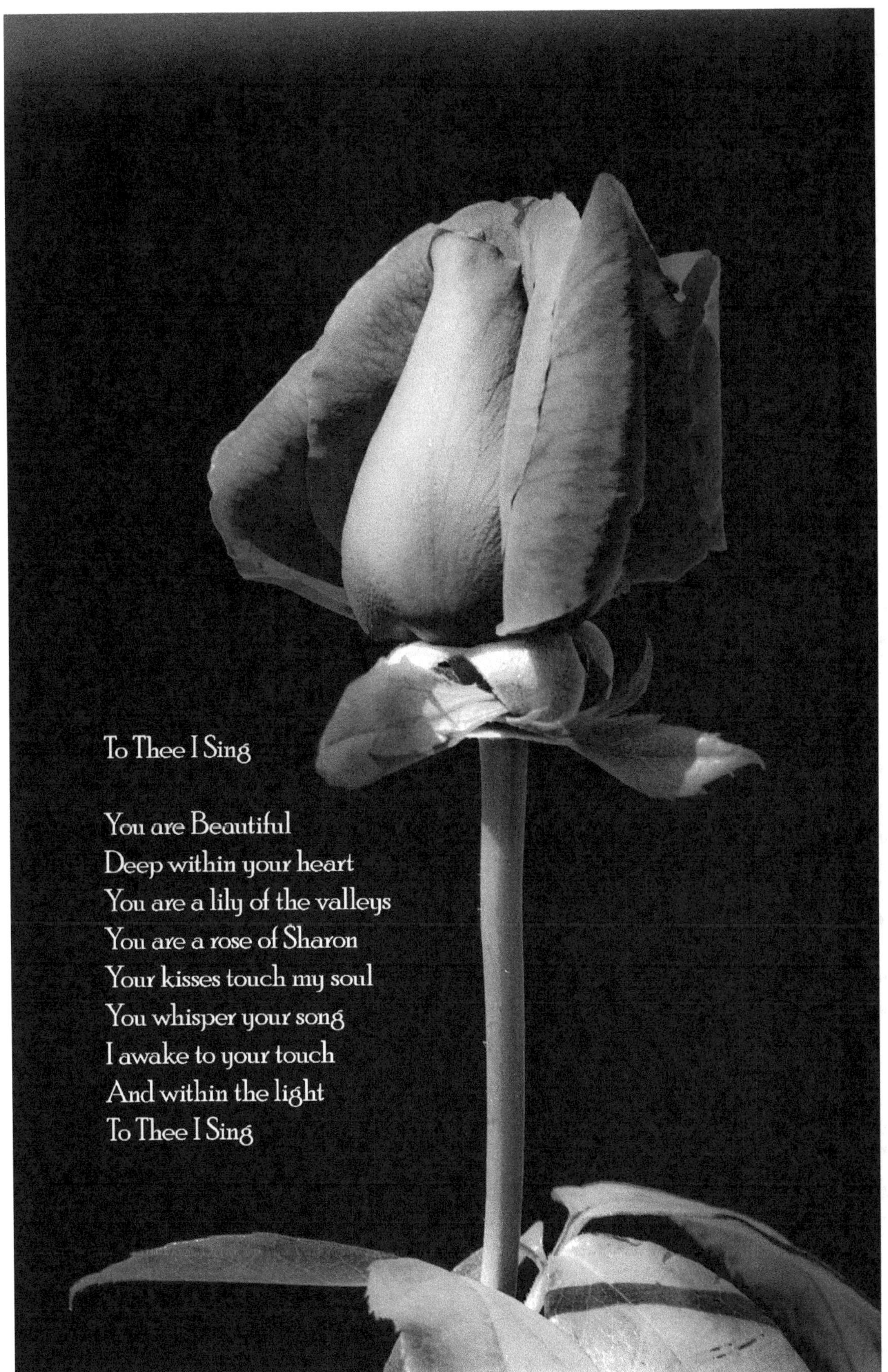
To Thee I Sing
You are Beautiful
Deep within your heart
You are a lily of the valleys
You are a rose of Sharon
Your kisses touch my soul
You whisper your song
I awake to your touch
And within the light
To Thee I Sing

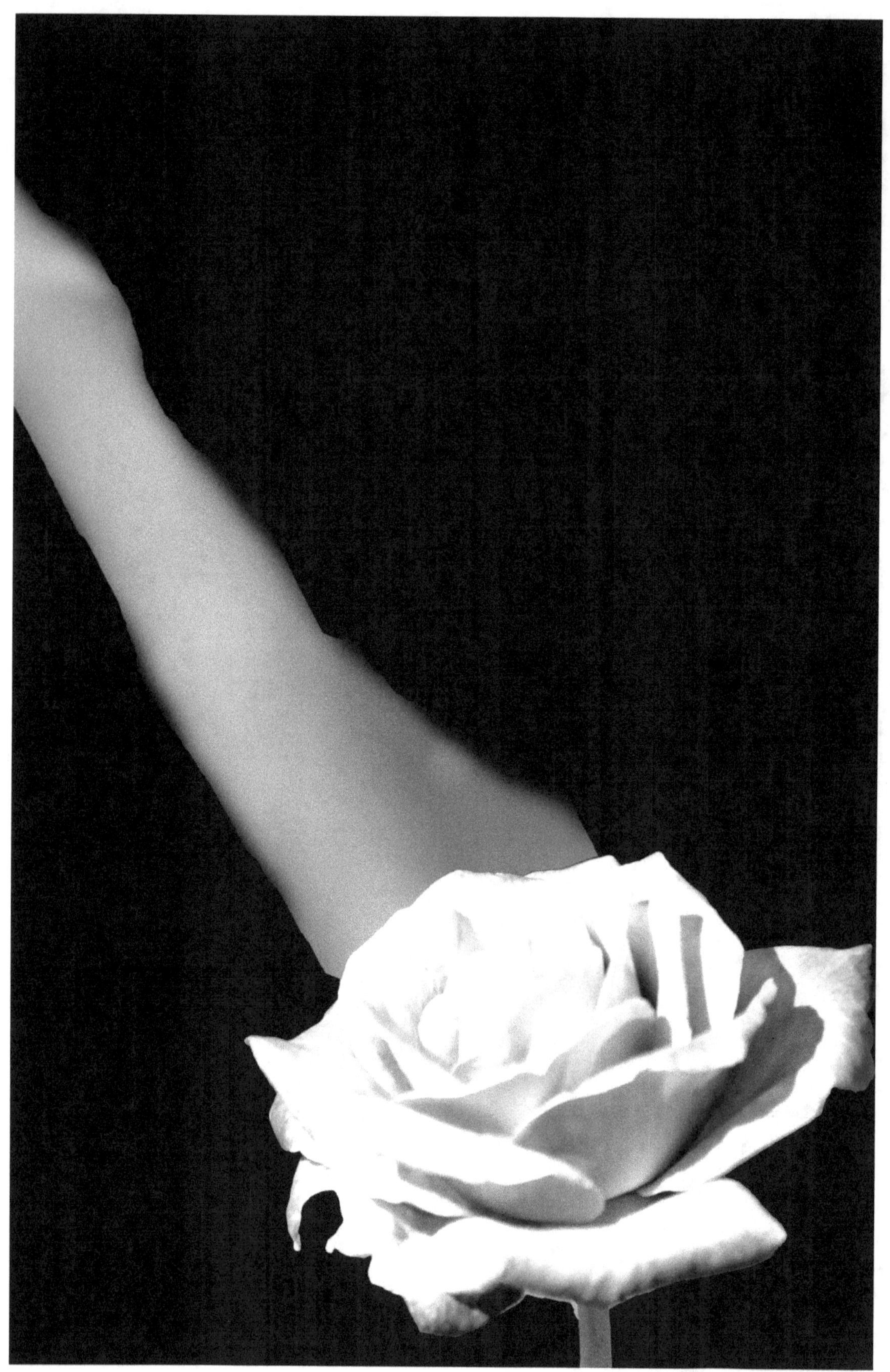

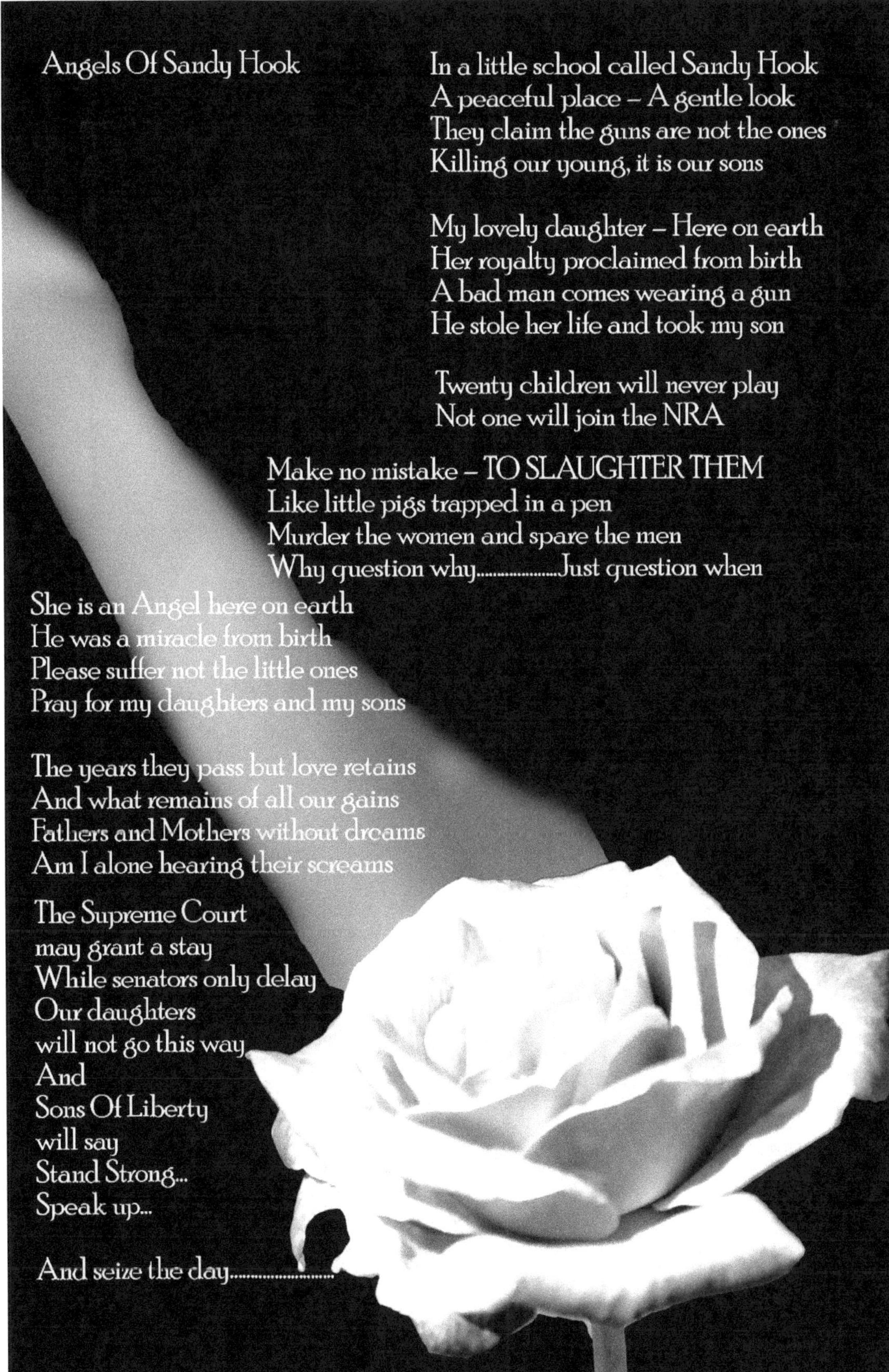

Angels Of Sandy Hook

In a little school called Sandy Hook
A peaceful place – A gentle look
They claim the guns are not the ones
Killing our young, it is our sons

My lovely daughter – Here on earth
Her royalty proclaimed from birth
A bad man comes wearing a gun
He stole her life and took my son

Twenty children will never play
Not one will join the NRA

Make no mistake – TO SLAUGHTER THEM
Like little pigs trapped in a pen
Murder the women and spare the men
Why question why..................Just question when

She is an Angel here on earth
He was a miracle from birth
Please suffer not the little ones
Pray for my daughters and my sons

The years they pass but love retains
And what remains of all our gains
Fathers and Mothers without dreams
Am I alone hearing their screams

The Supreme Court
may grant a stay
While senators only delay
Our daughters
will not go this way
And
Sons Of Liberty
will say
Stand Strong...
Speak up...

And seize the day.........................

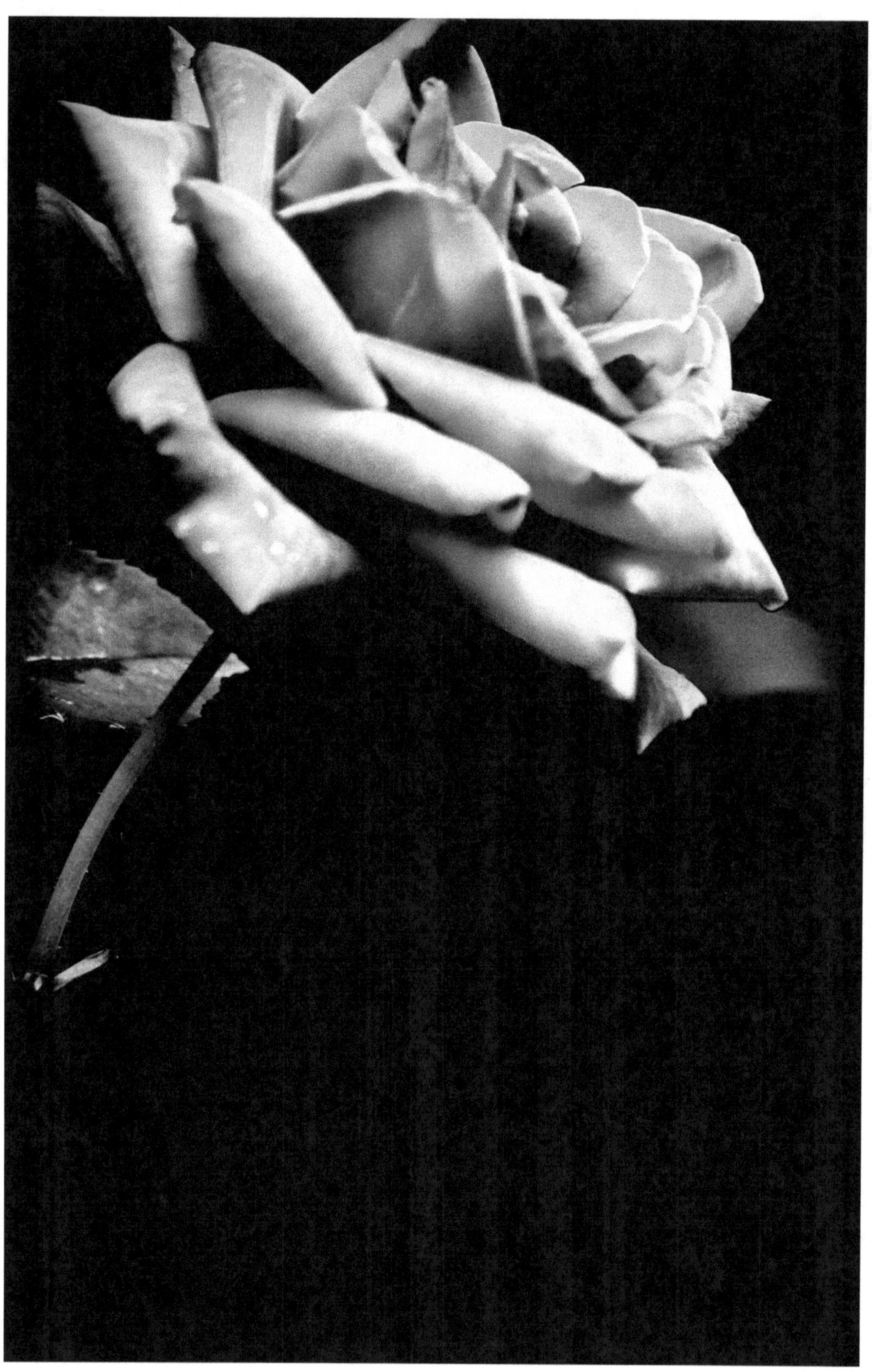

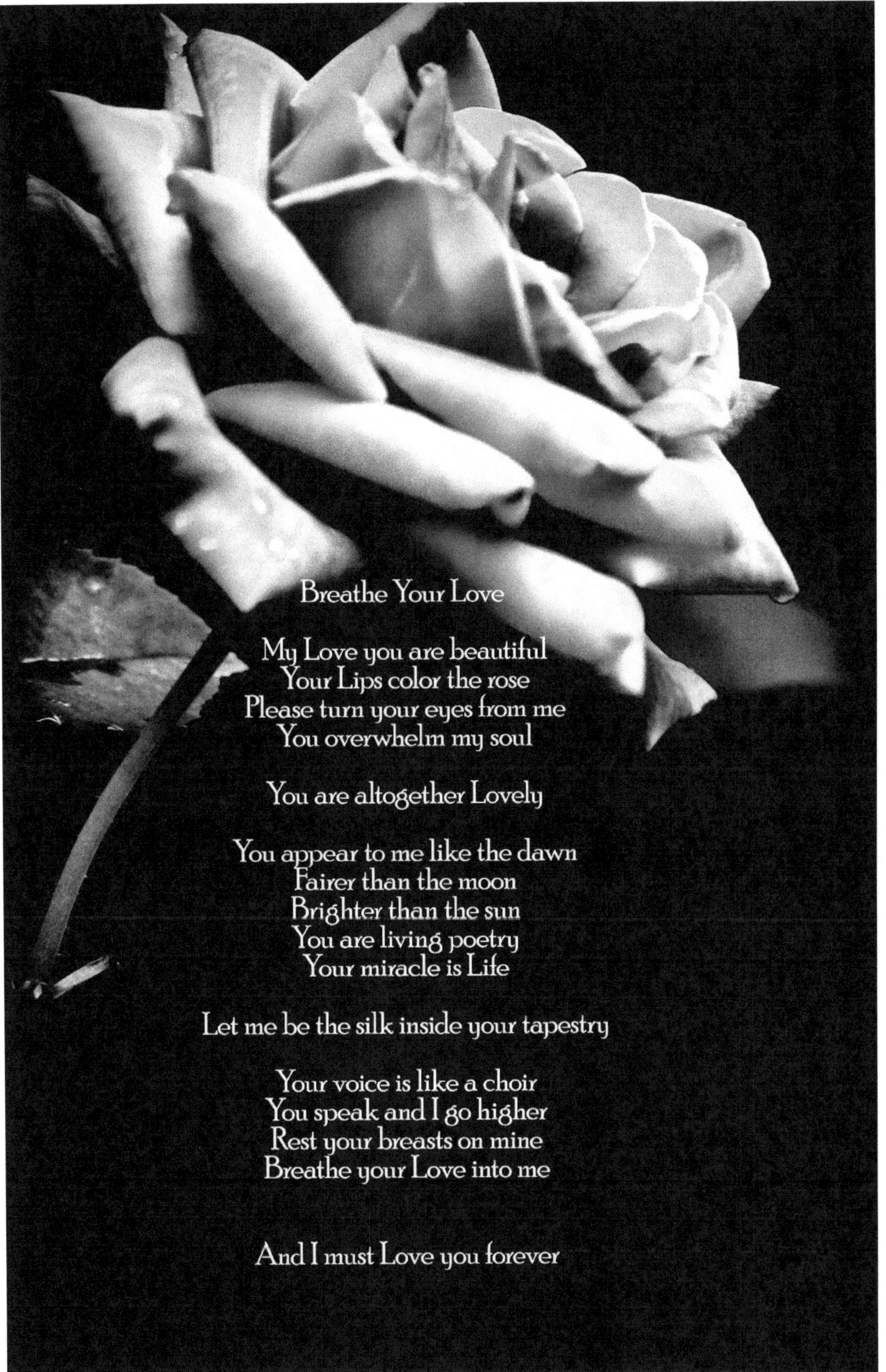
Breathe Your Love

My Love you are beautiful
Your Lips color the rose
Please turn your eyes from me
You overwhelm my soul

You are altogether Lovely

You appear to me like the dawn
Fairer than the moon
Brighter than the sun
You are living poetry
Your miracle is Life

Let me be the silk inside your tapestry

Your voice is like a choir
You speak and I go higher
Rest your breasts on mine
Breathe your Love into me

And I must Love you forever

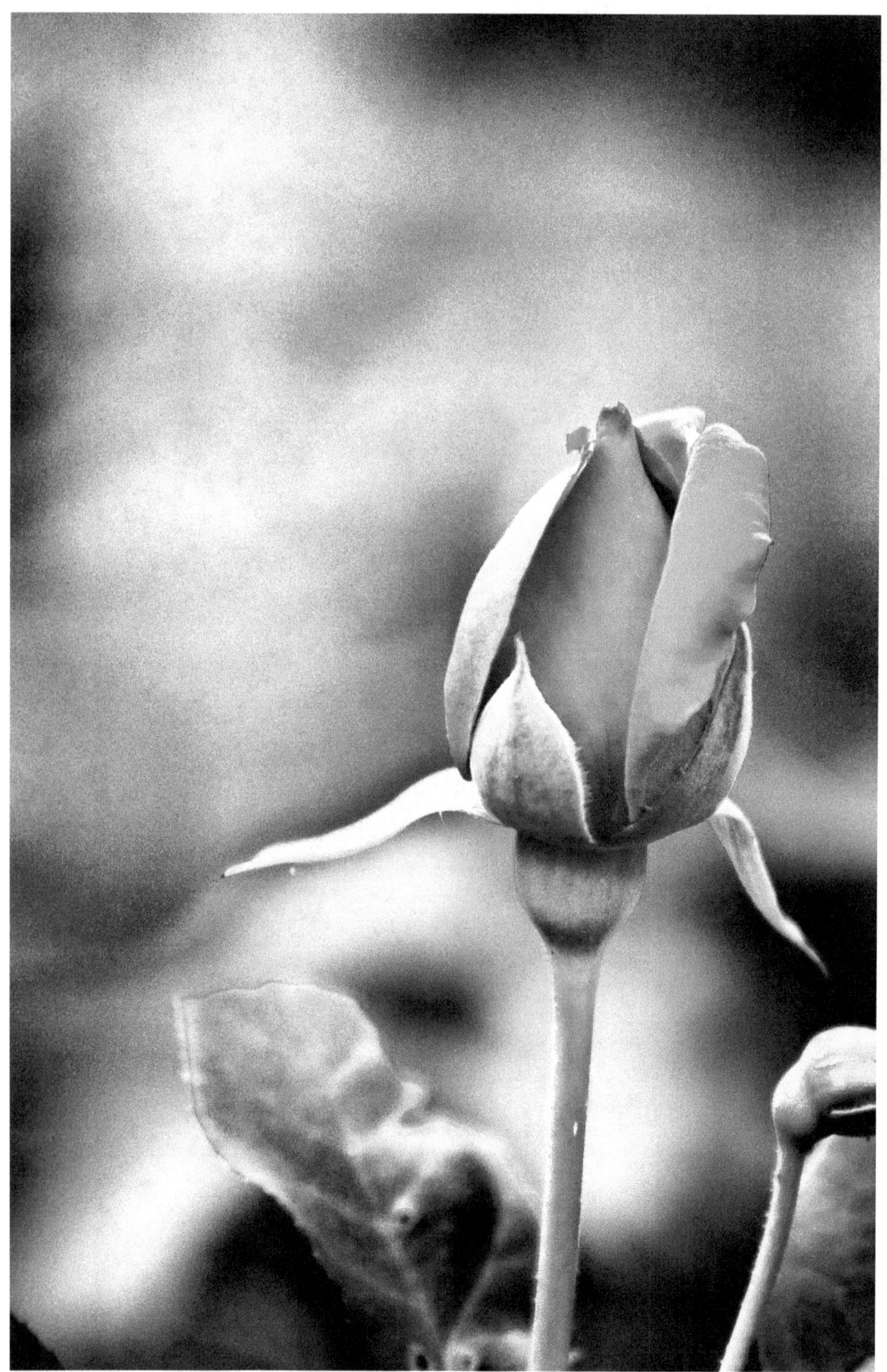

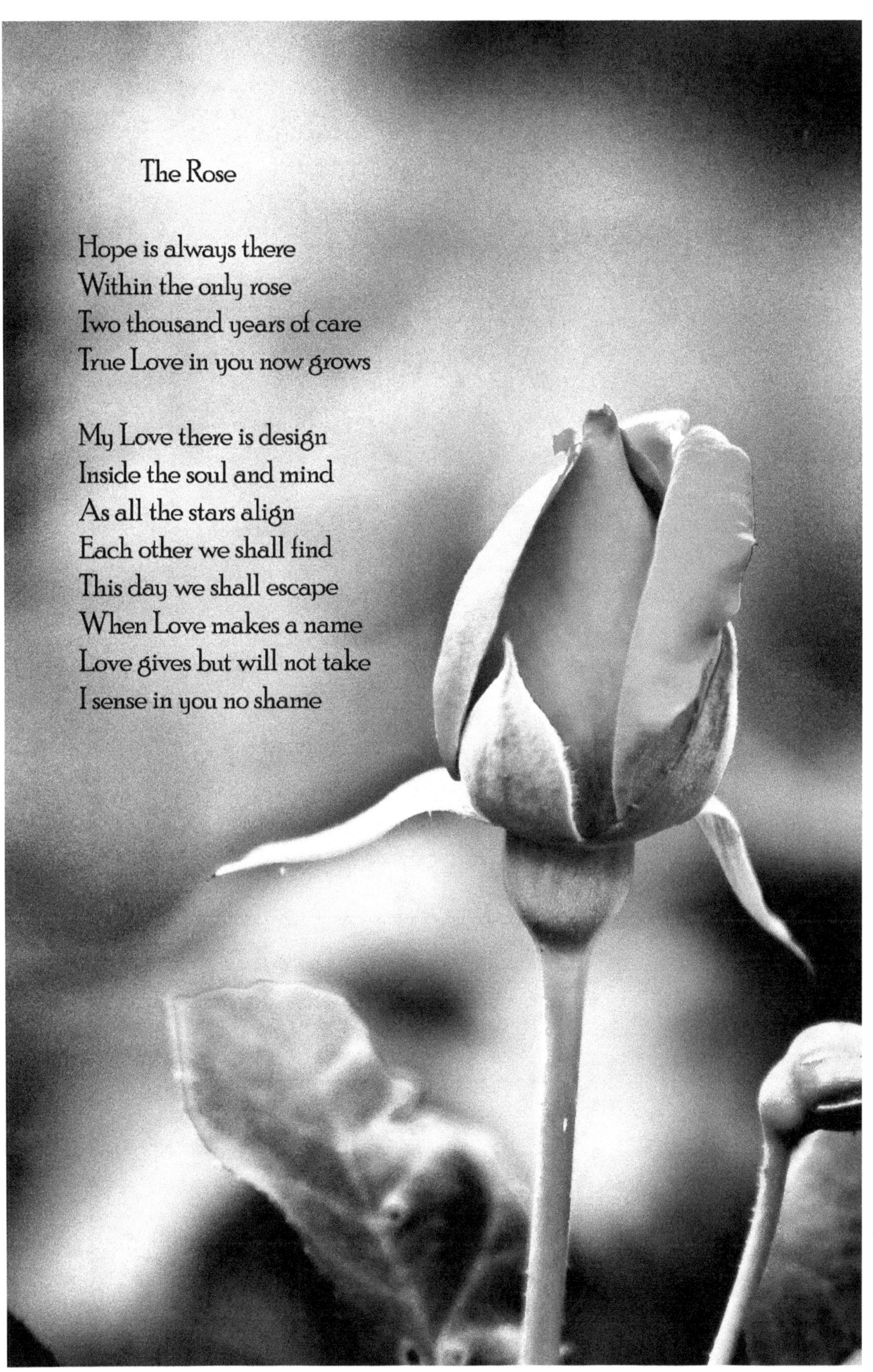

The Rose

Hope is always there
Within the only rose
Two thousand years of care
True Love in you now grows

My Love there is design
Inside the soul and mind
As all the stars align
Each other we shall find
This day we shall escape
When Love makes a name
Love gives but will not take
I sense in you no shame

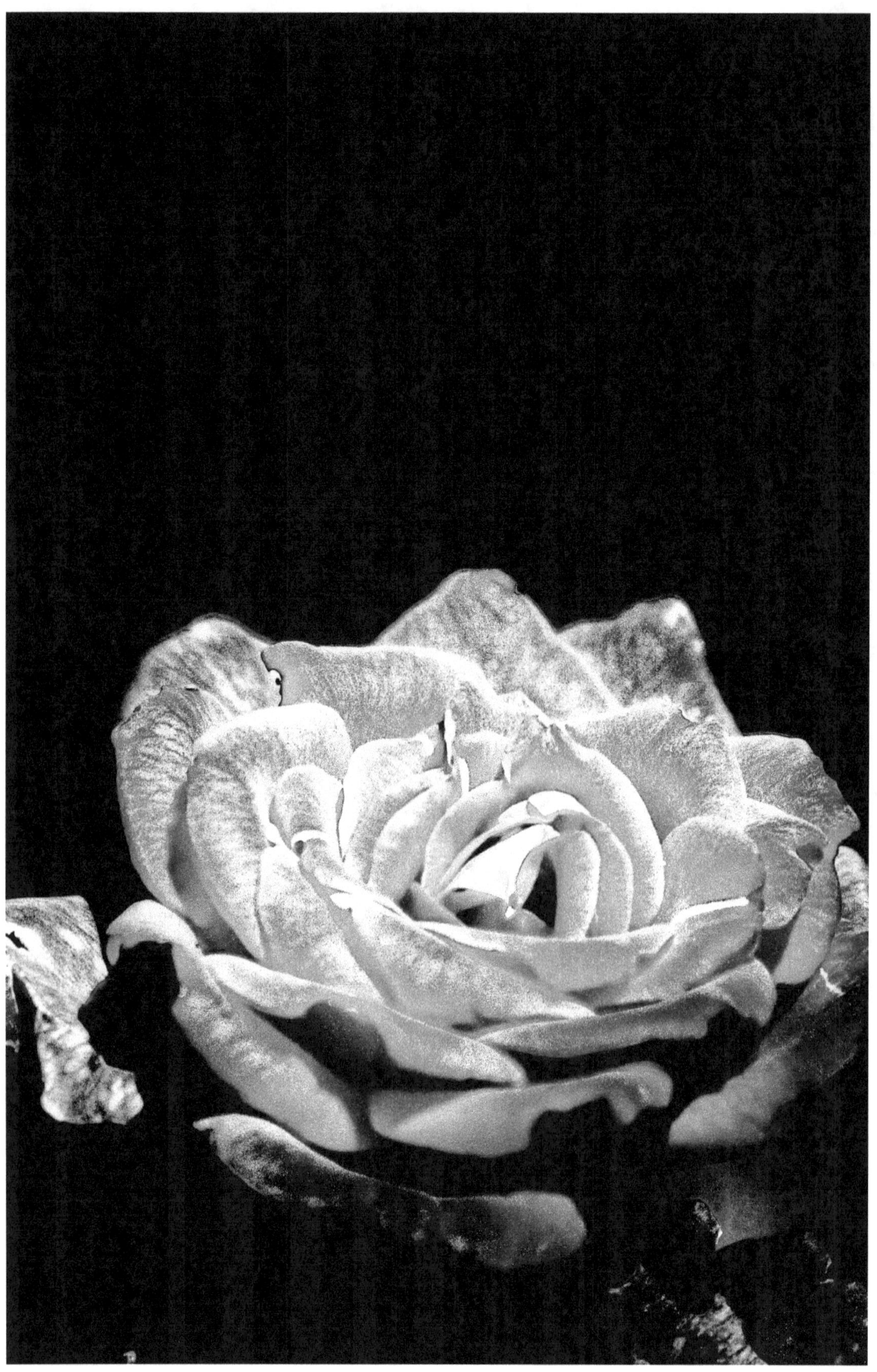

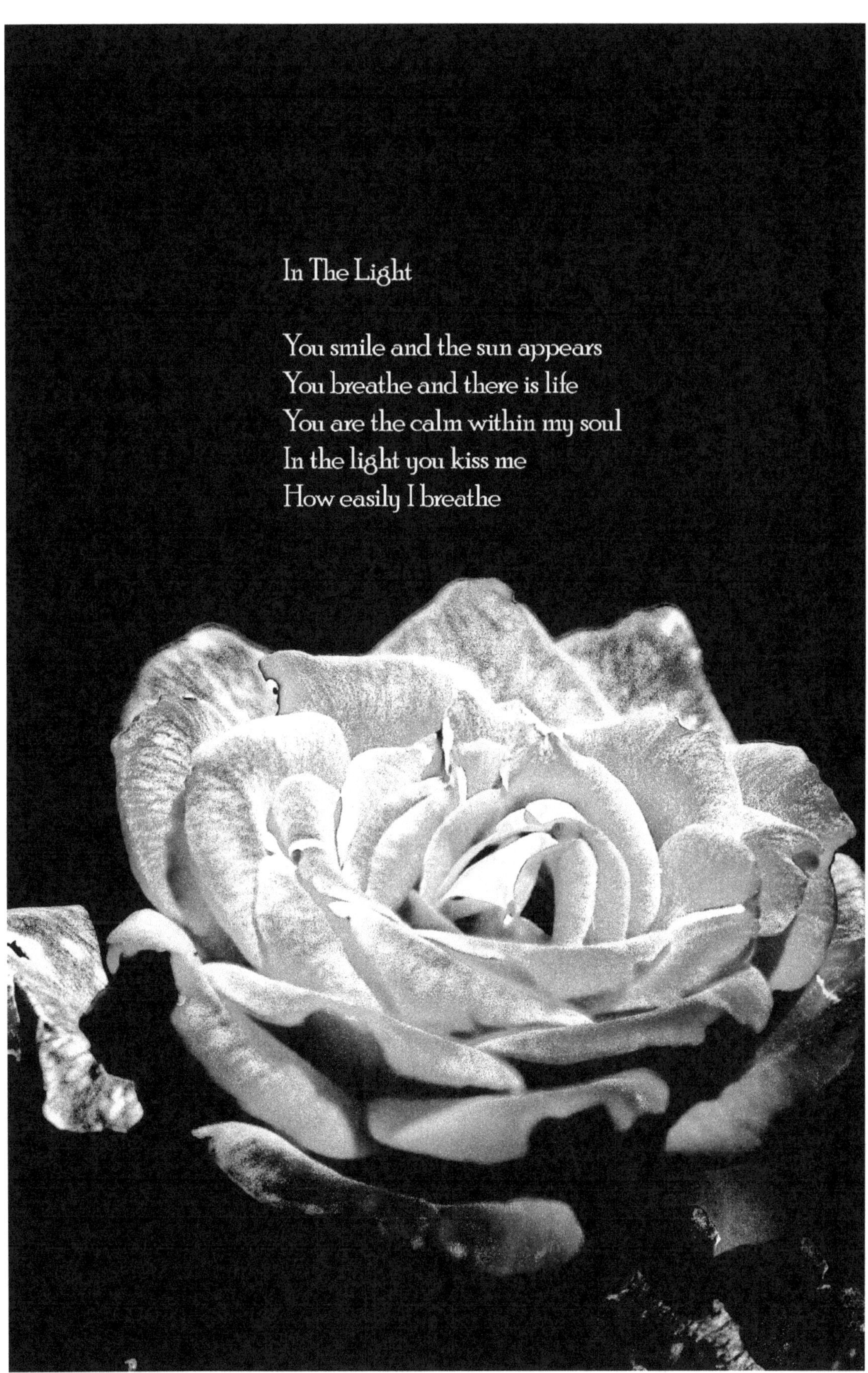

In The Light

You smile and the sun appears
You breathe and there is life
You are the calm within my soul
In the light you kiss me
How easily I breathe

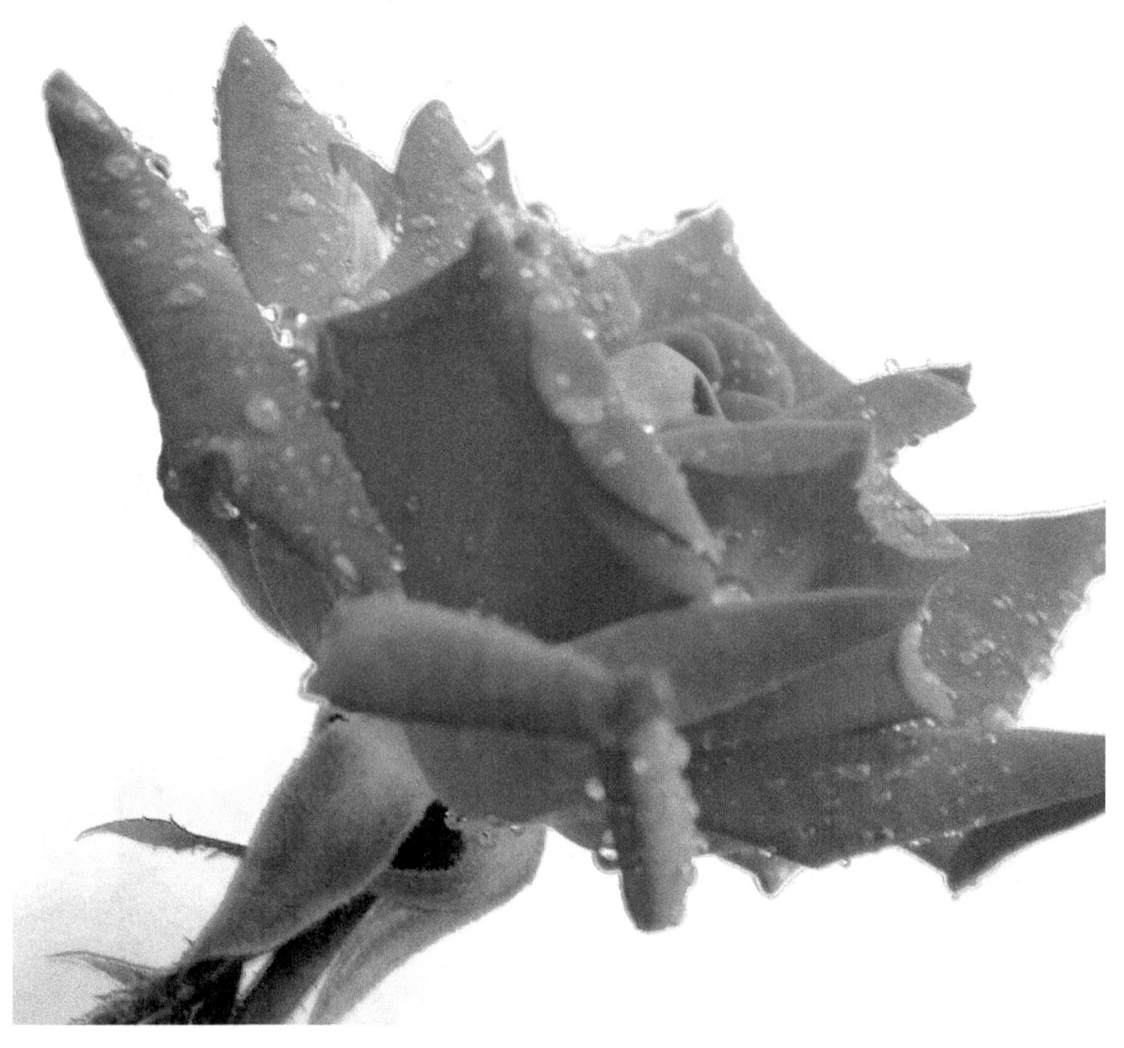

Love Lightly Lies

Living in each moment
Your words are kind and true
To me you sing of simple things
Like the laughter in you

Purity in giving
Nor driven by their greed
You give to all without recall
Gently planting a seed

To end is the beginning
Love lightly lies inside
So sing and let the heavens ring
In you the dew resides

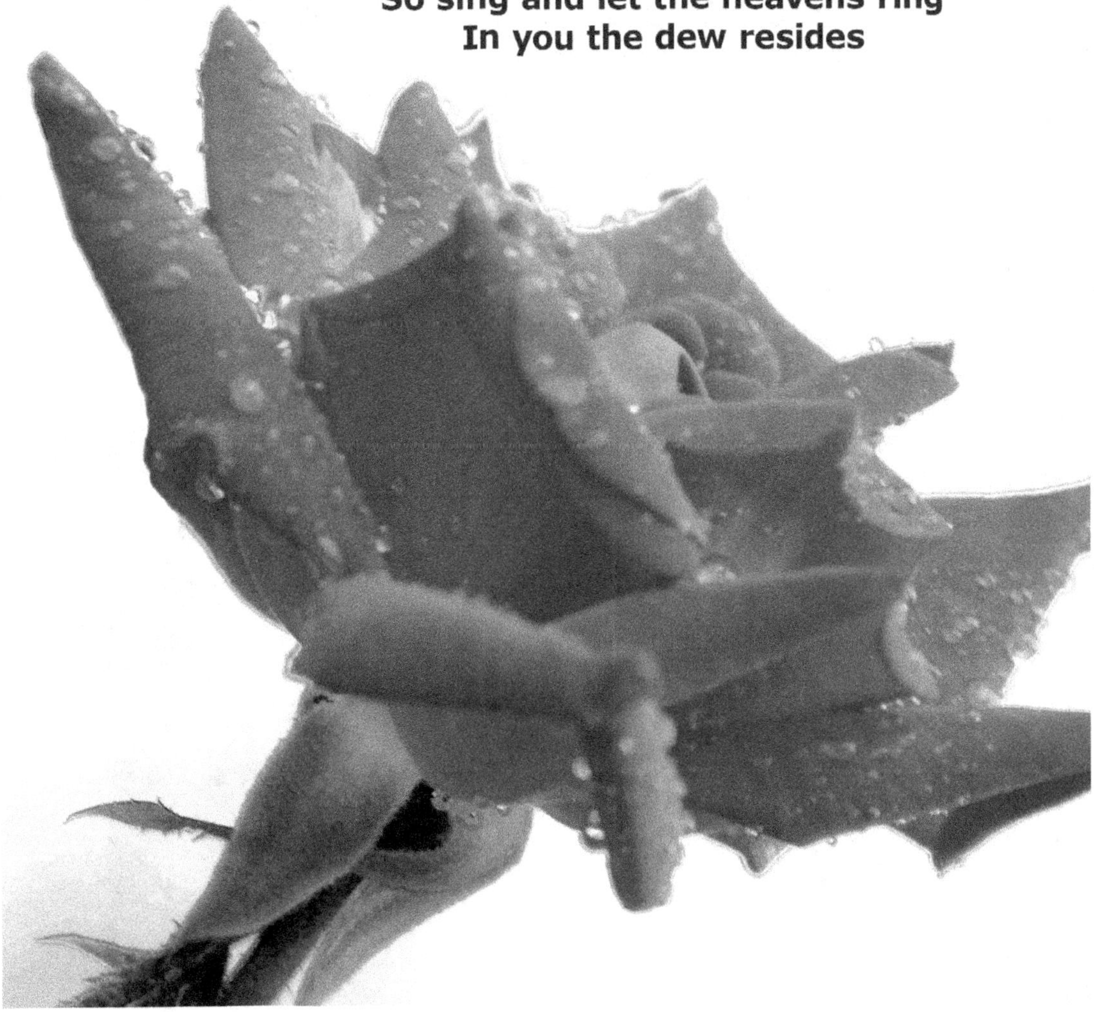

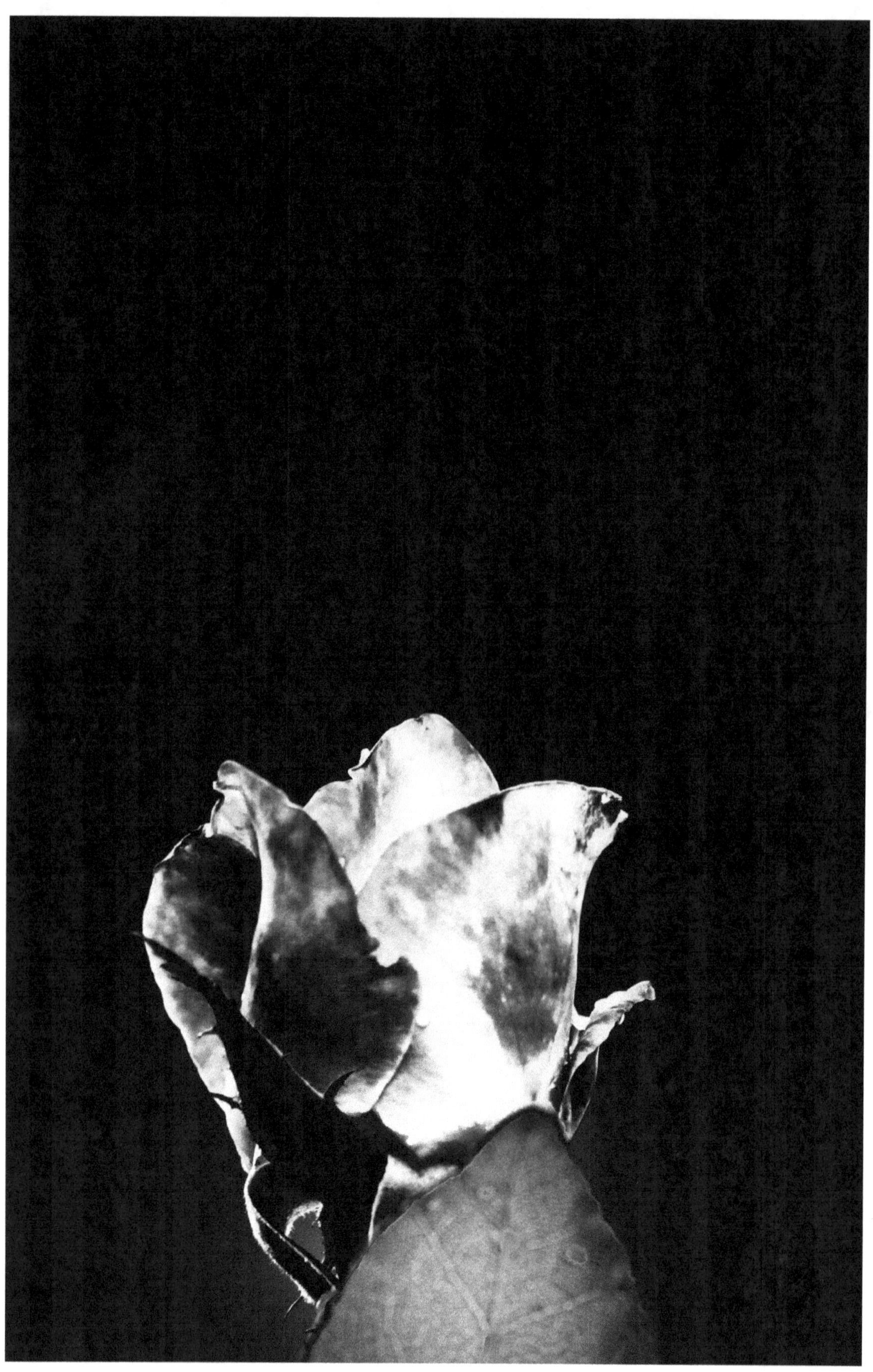

Promised Lands

Our lips have touched a million times
In passions gentle refrain

Our bodies entwine under the sun
And In the soothing rain

Your eyes outshine the universe
My heart beats in your hands

My Love when I am inside of you
I have reached the promised lands

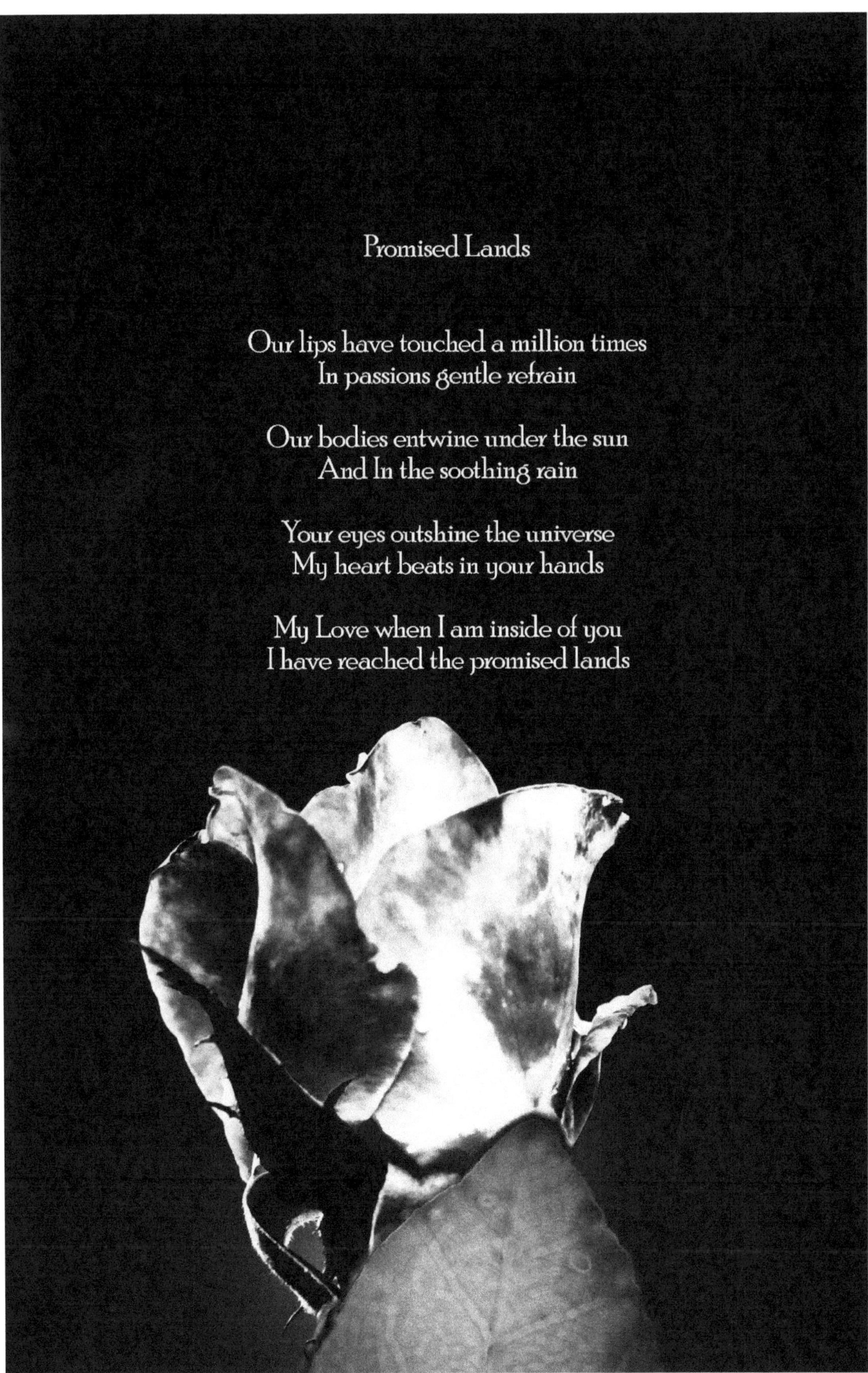

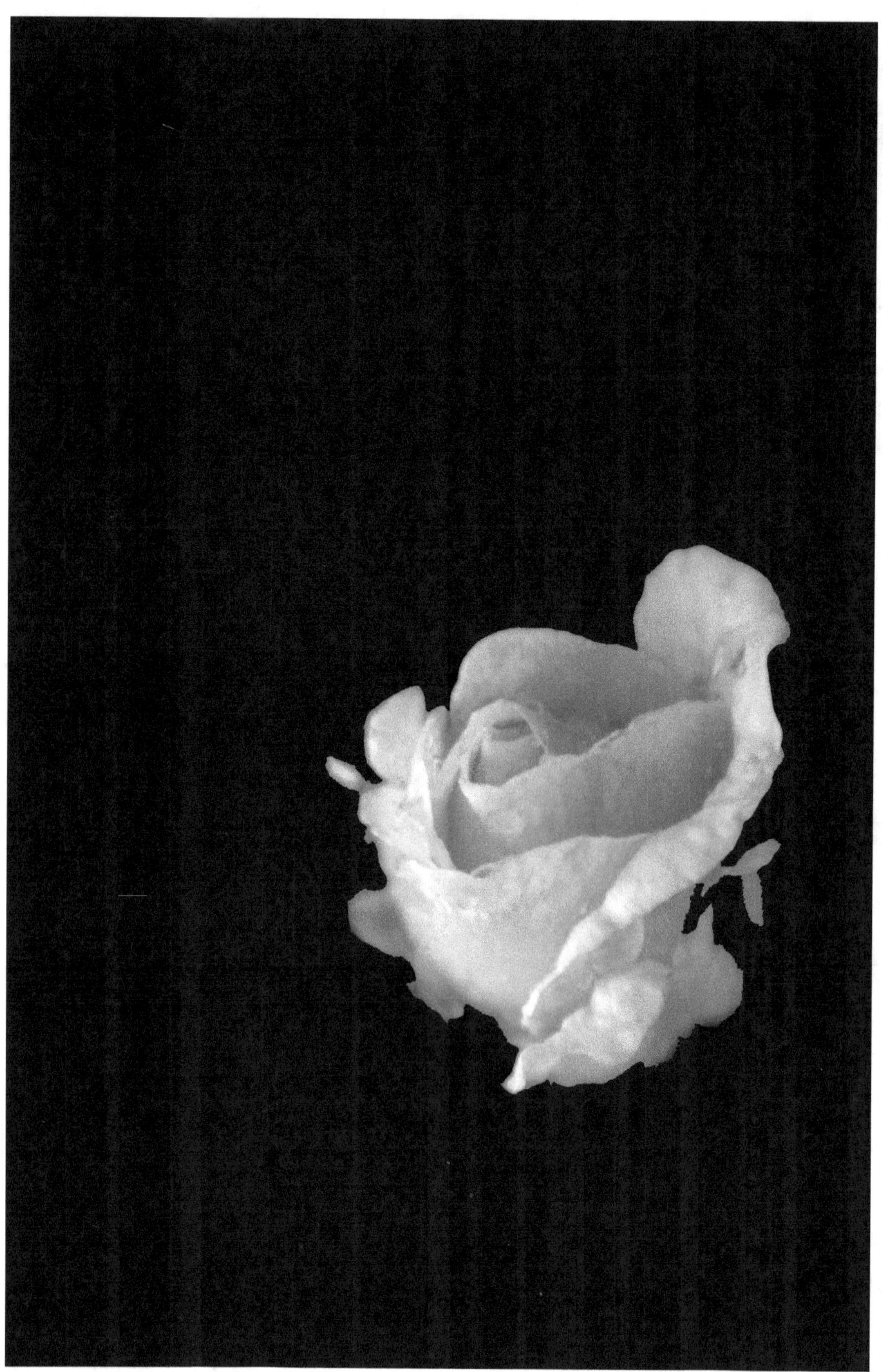

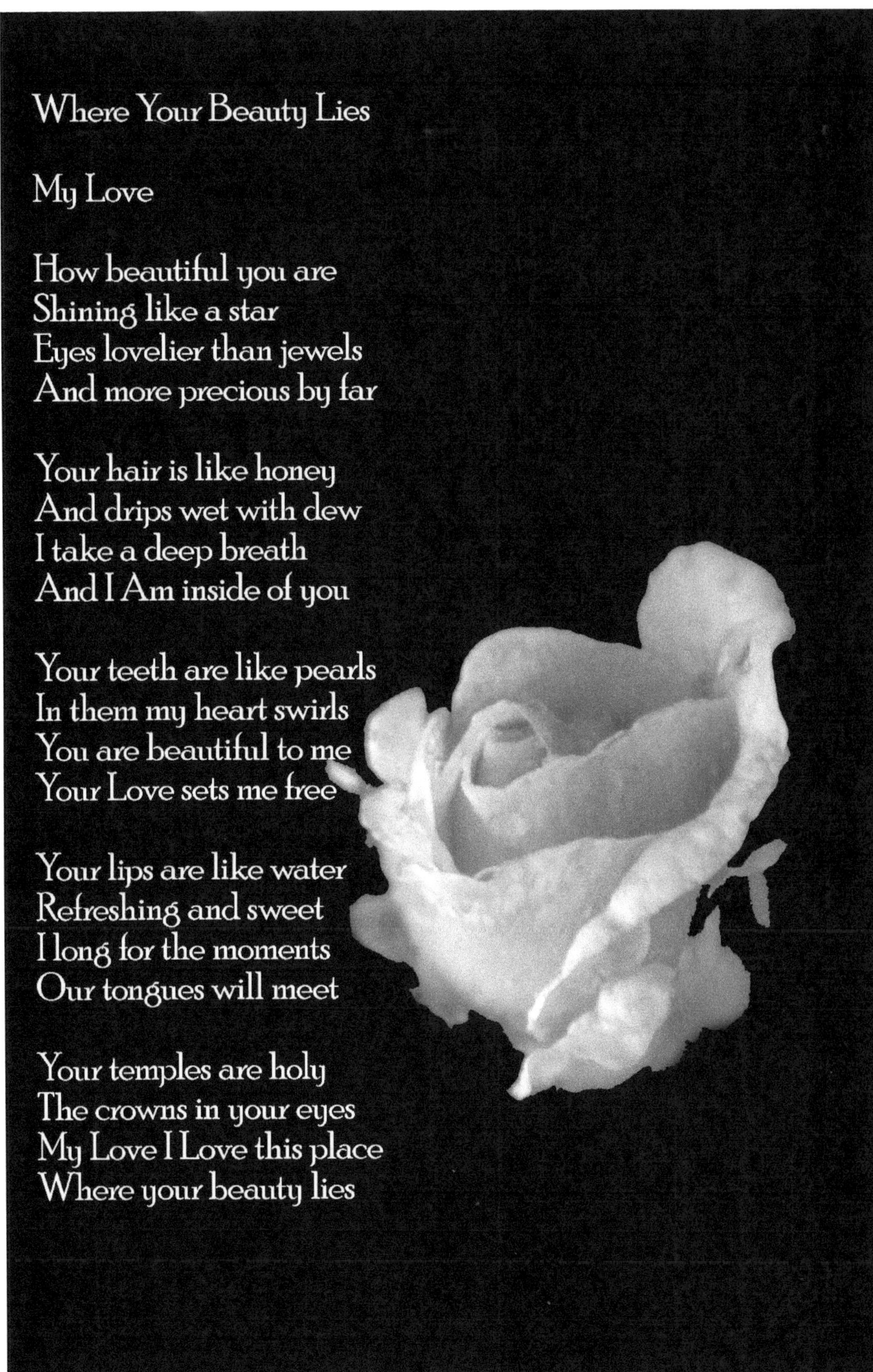

Where Your Beauty Lies

My Love

How beautiful you are
Shining like a star
Eyes lovelier than jewels
And more precious by far

Your hair is like honey
And drips wet with dew
I take a deep breath
And I Am inside of you

Your teeth are like pearls
In them my heart swirls
You are beautiful to me
Your Love sets me free

Your lips are like water
Refreshing and sweet
I long for the moments
Our tongues will meet

Your temples are holy
The crowns in your eyes
My Love I Love this place
Where your beauty lies

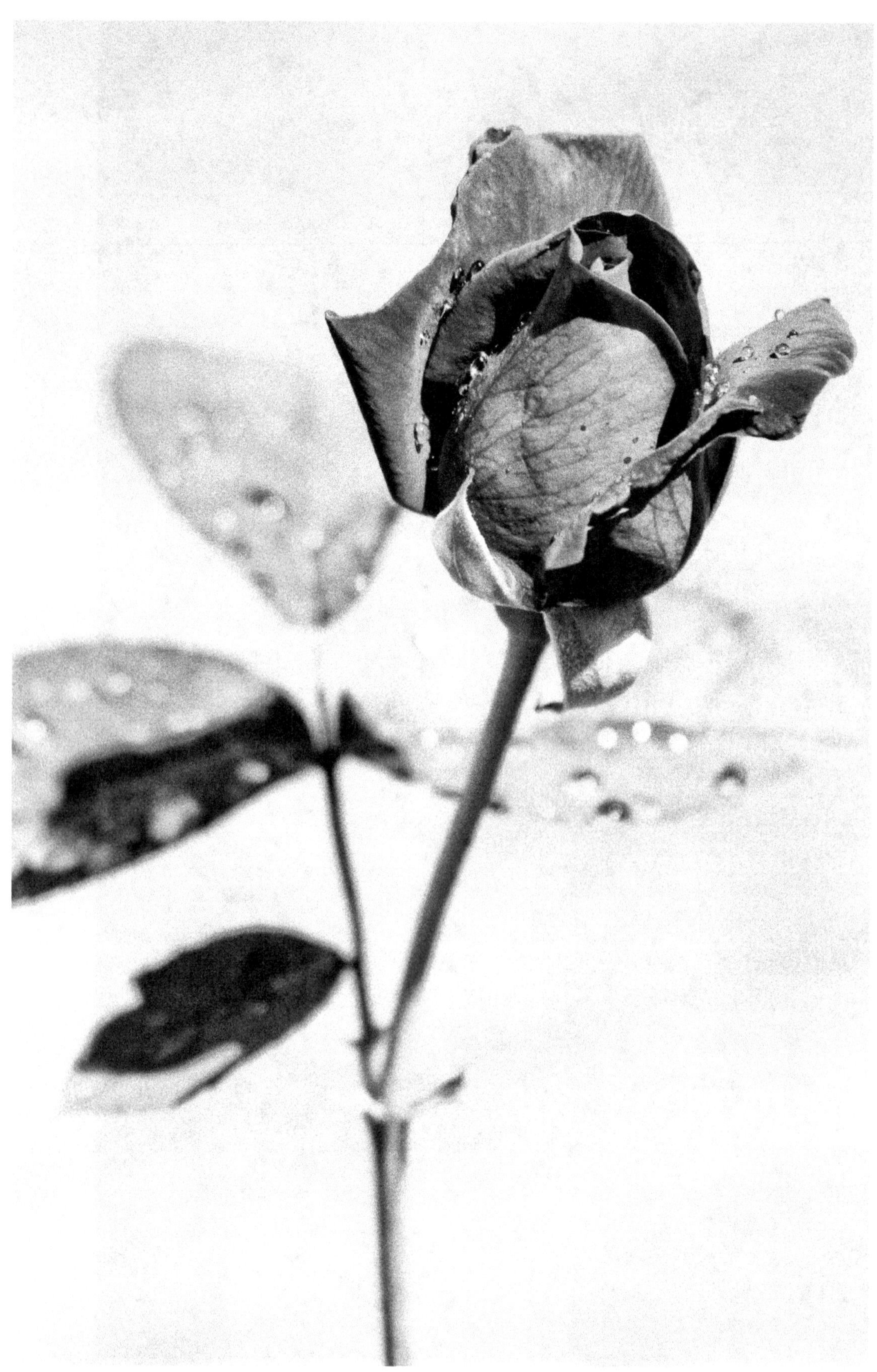

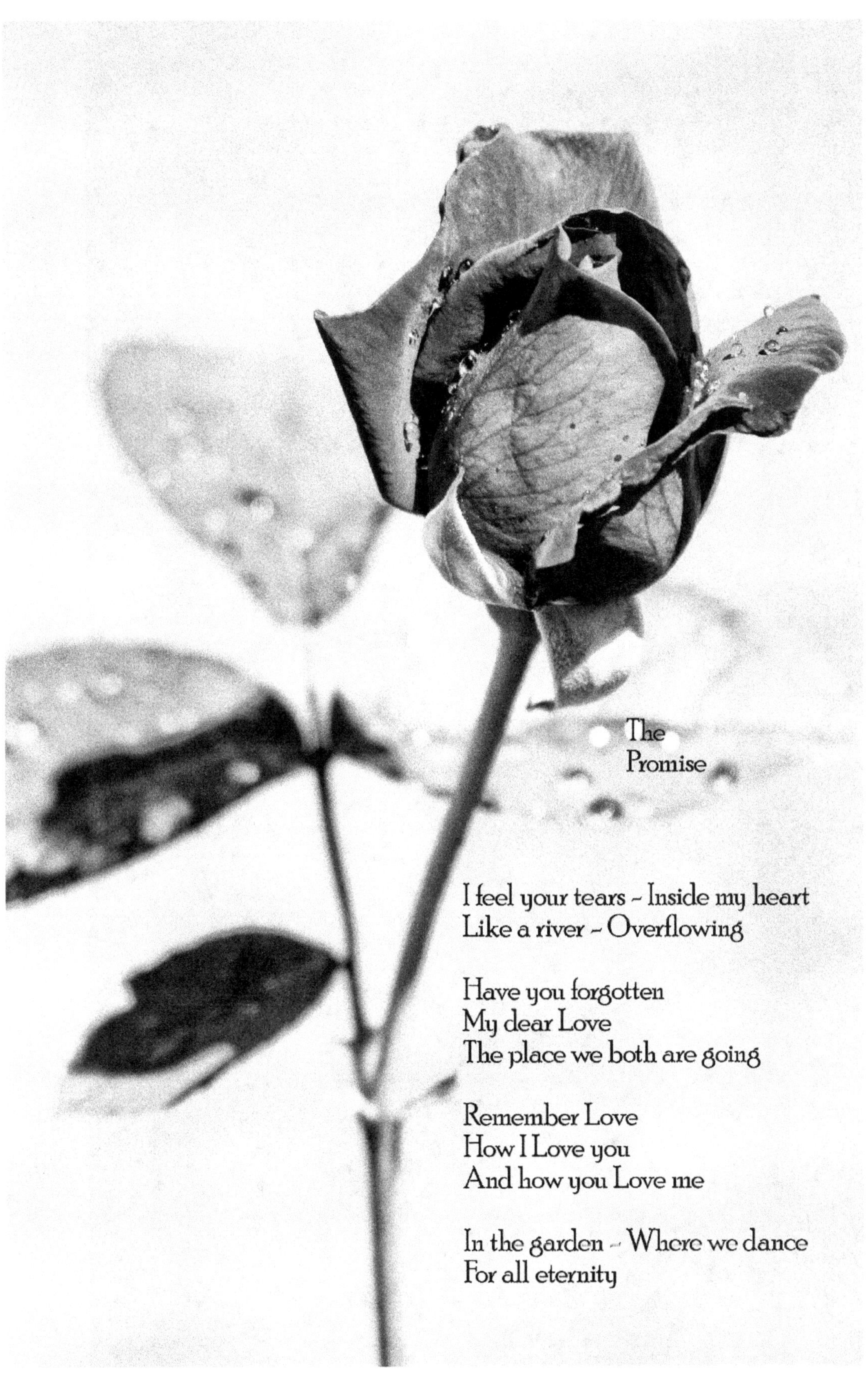

The Promise

I feel your tears – Inside my heart
Like a river – Overflowing

Have you forgotten
My dear Love
The place we both are going

Remember Love
How I Love you
And how you Love me

In the garden – Where we dance
For all eternity

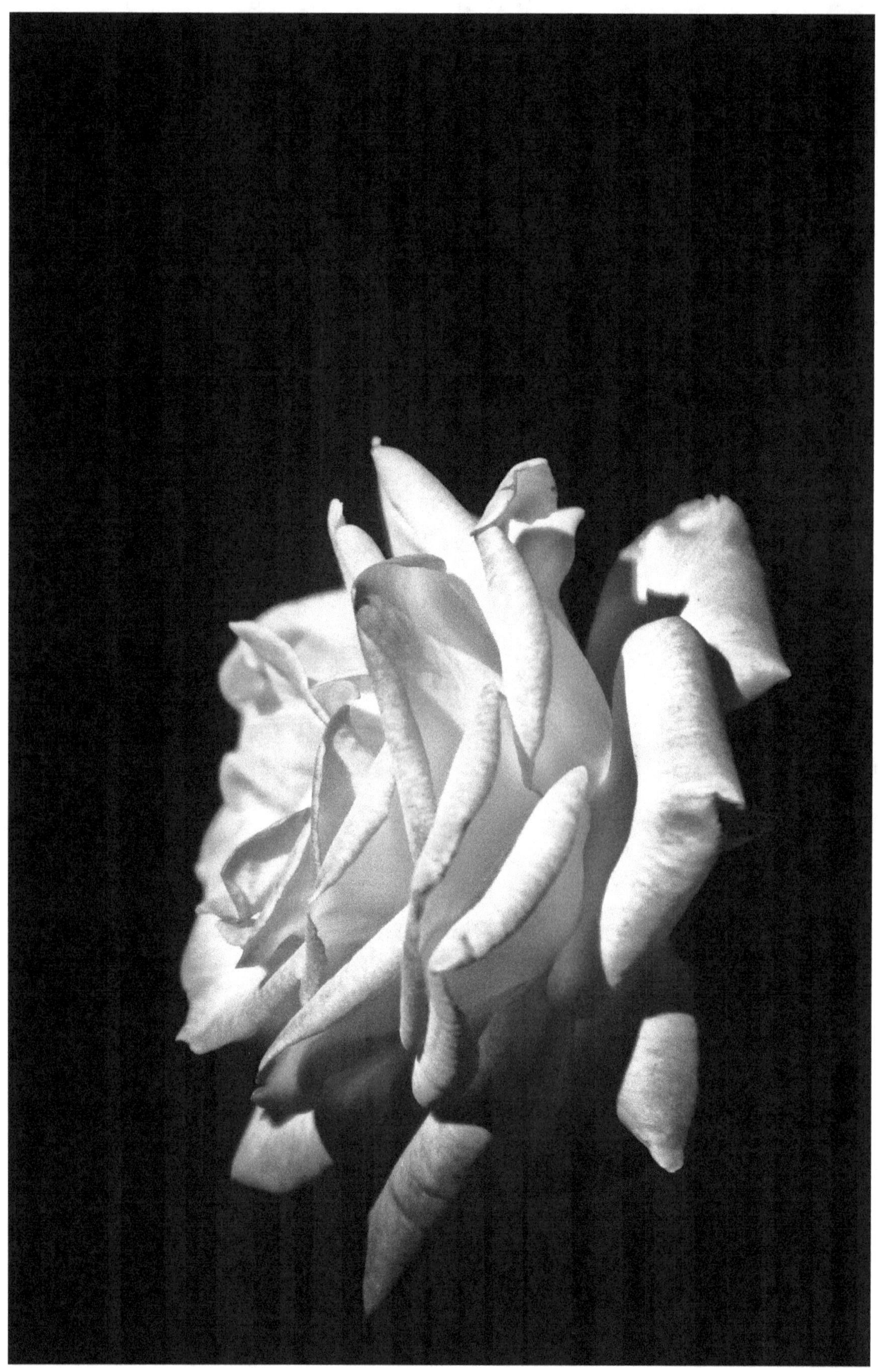

I Know

When I give to you my heart
I hope you will be kind
I know you know this is true
True Love is hard to find

Maybe the reason this is so
Love is a seed for two
Each caring will let Love grow
Alone and Love will go

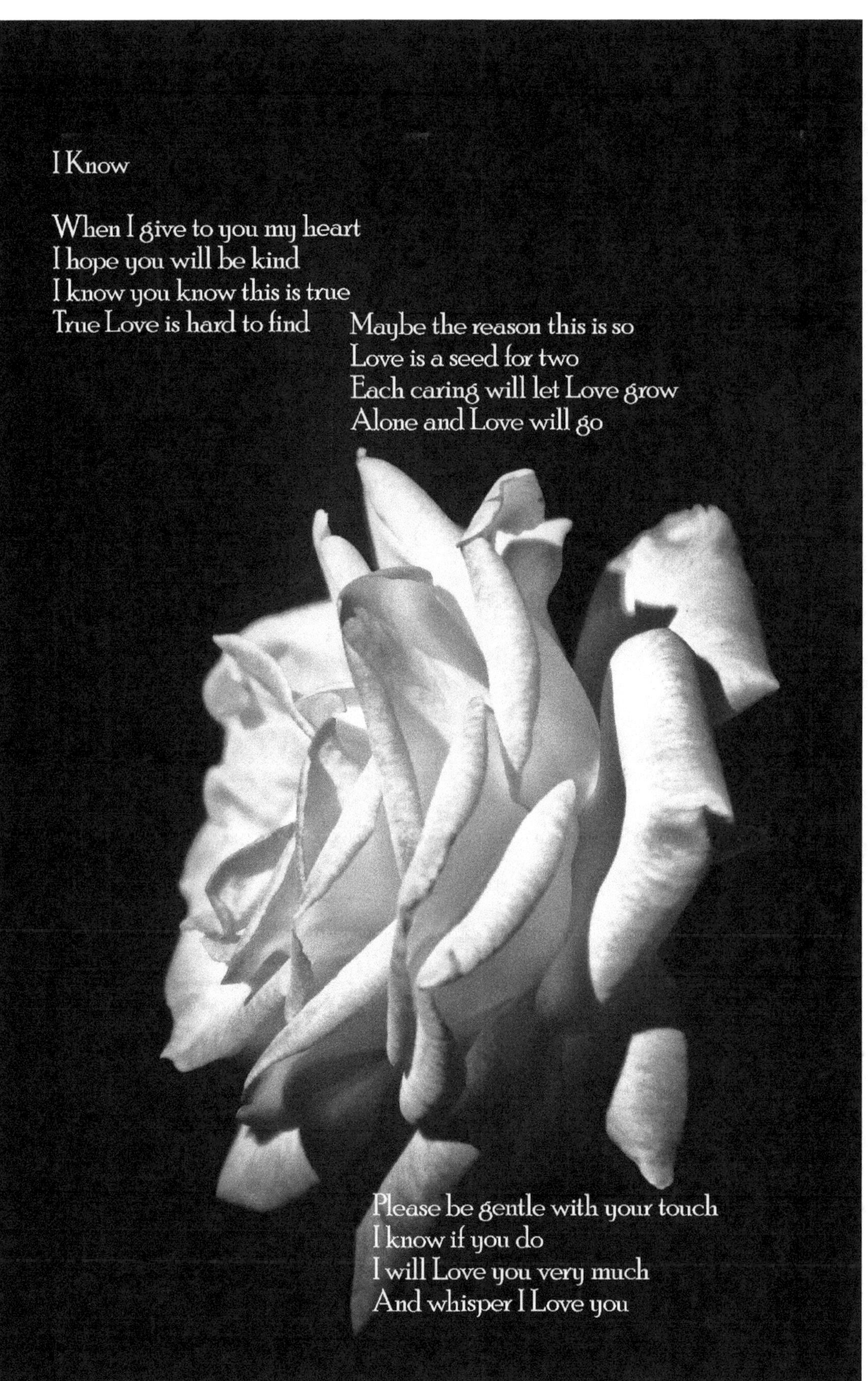

Please be gentle with your touch
I know if you do
I will Love you very much
And whisper I Love you

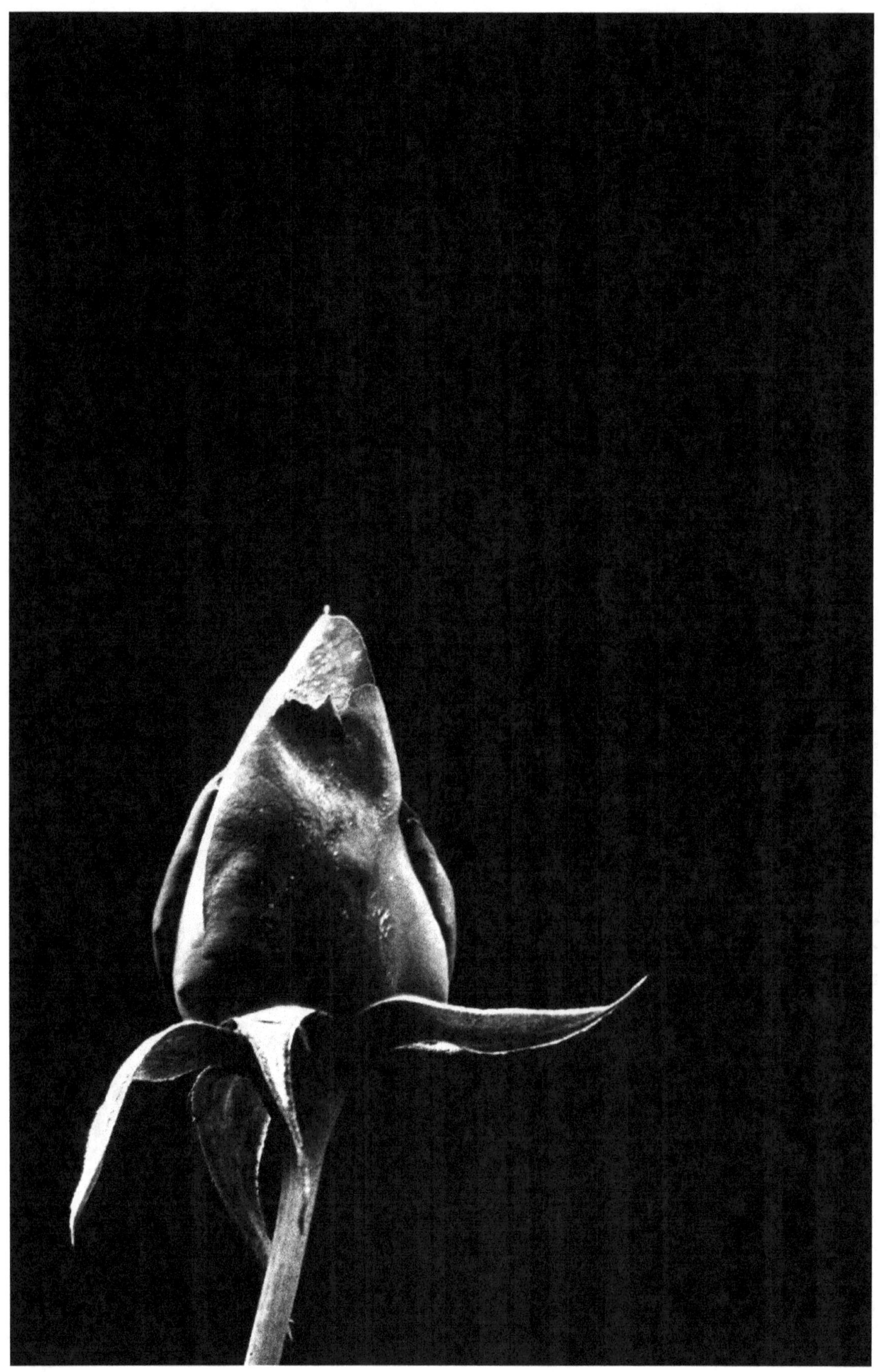

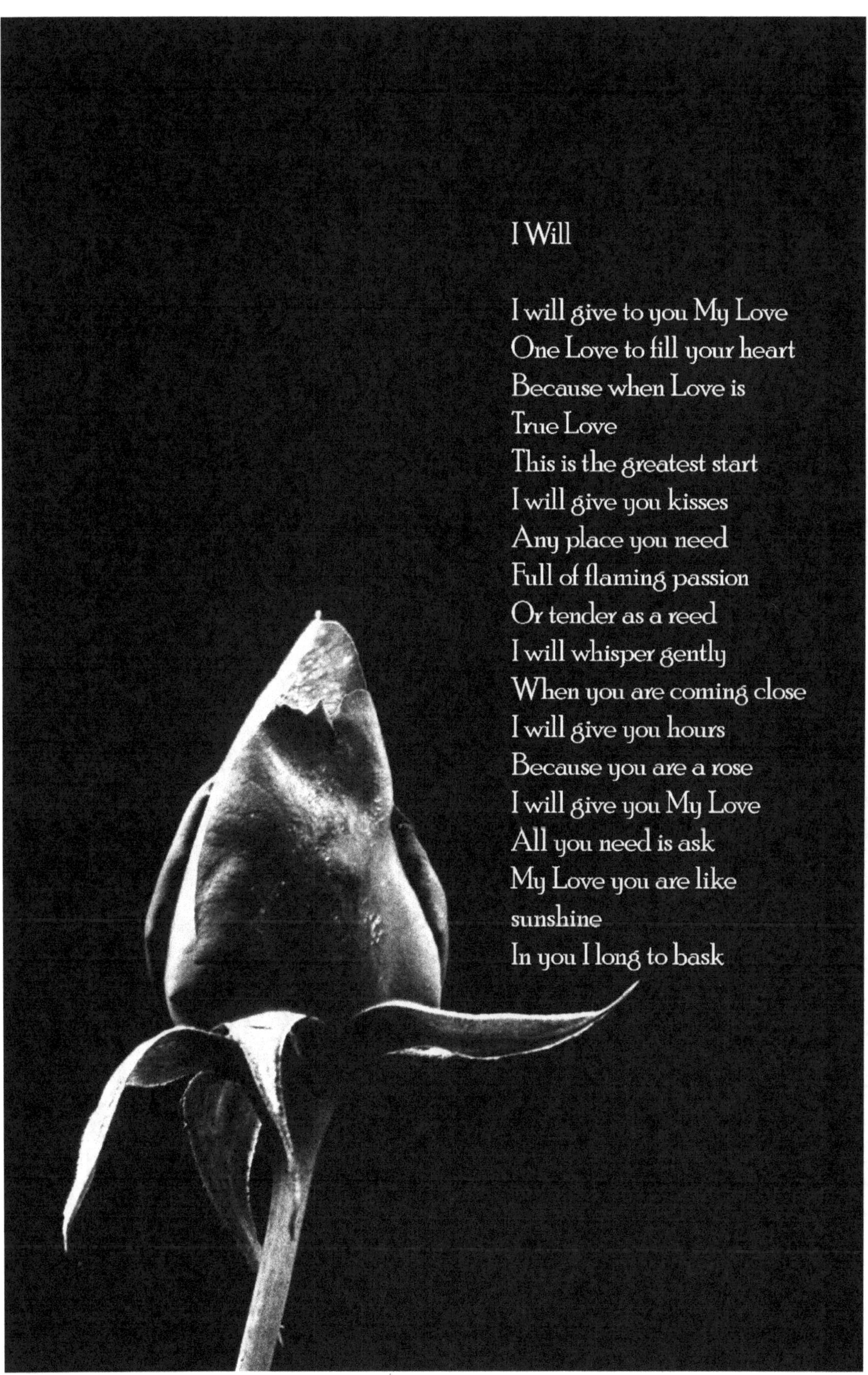

I Will

I will give to you My Love
One Love to fill your heart
Because when Love is
True Love
This is the greatest start
I will give you kisses
Any place you need
Full of flaming passion
Or tender as a reed
I will whisper gently
When you are coming close
I will give you hours
Because you are a rose
I will give you My Love
All you need is ask
My Love you are like
sunshine
In you I long to bask

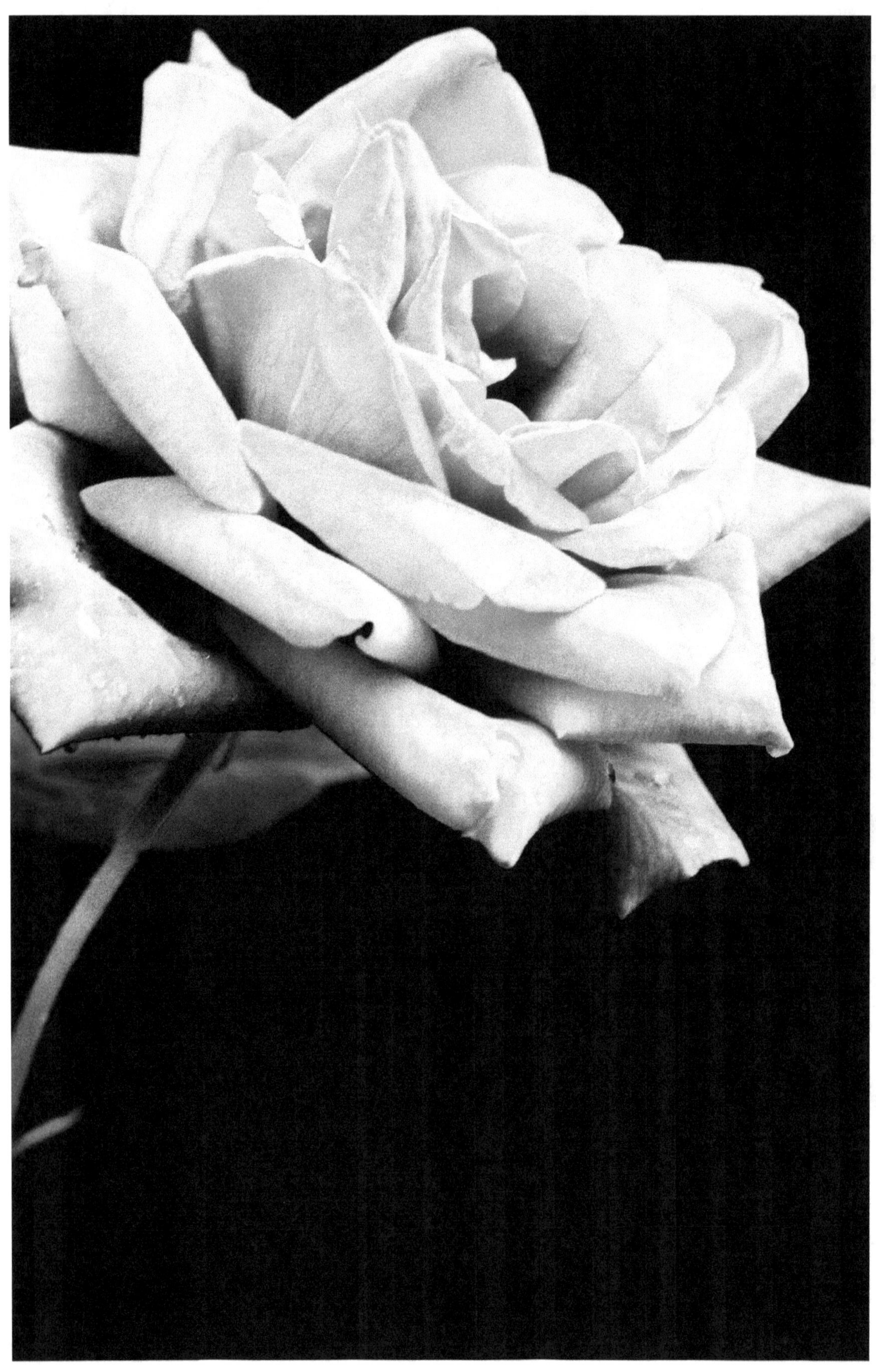

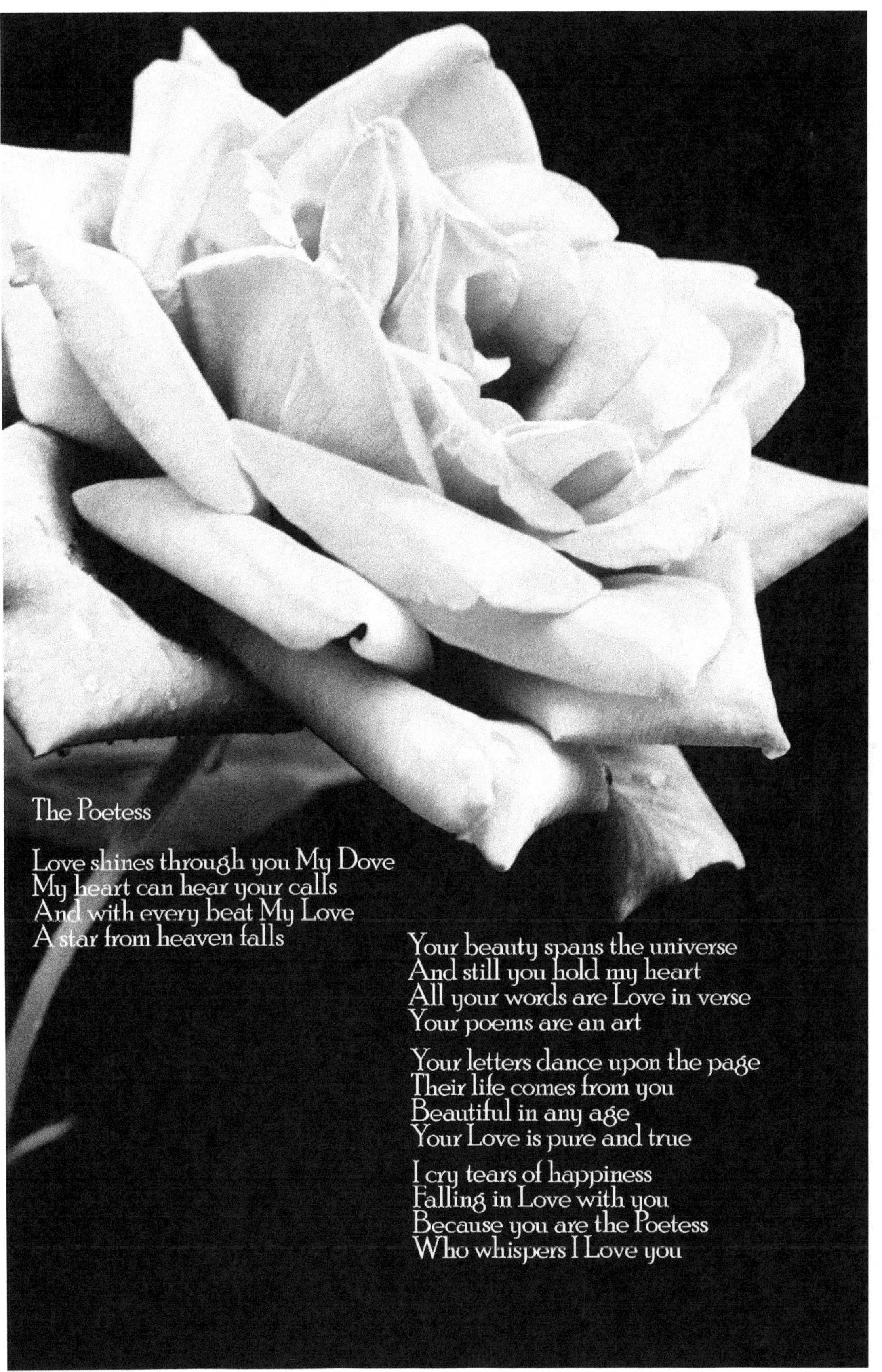
The Poetess

Love shines through you My Dove
My heart can hear your calls
And with every beat My Love
A star from heaven falls

Your beauty spans the universe
And still you hold my heart
All your words are Love in verse
Your poems are an art

Your letters dance upon the page
Their life comes from you
Beautiful in any age
Your Love is pure and true

I cry tears of happiness
Falling in Love with you
Because you are the Poetess
Who whispers I Love you

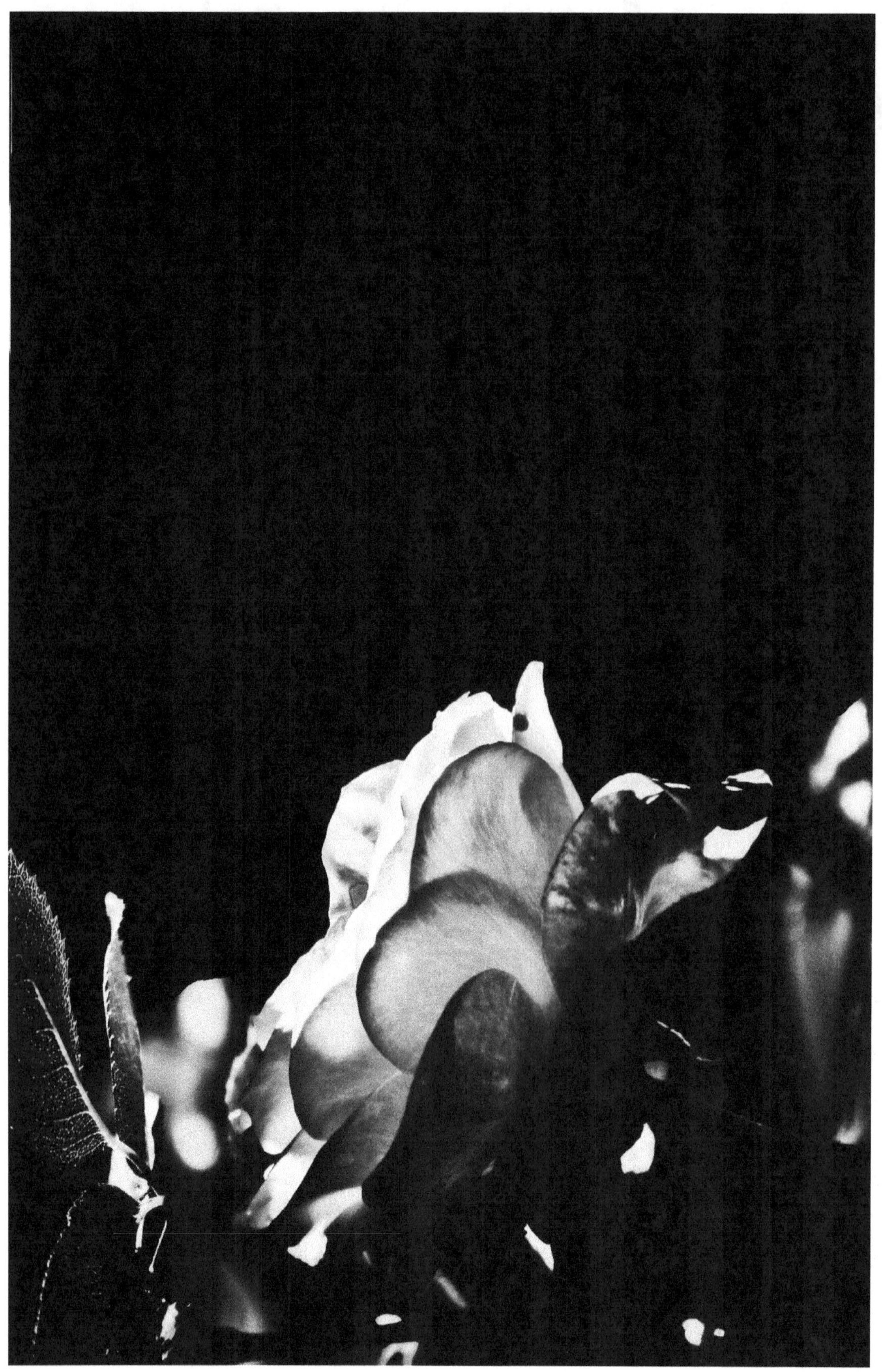

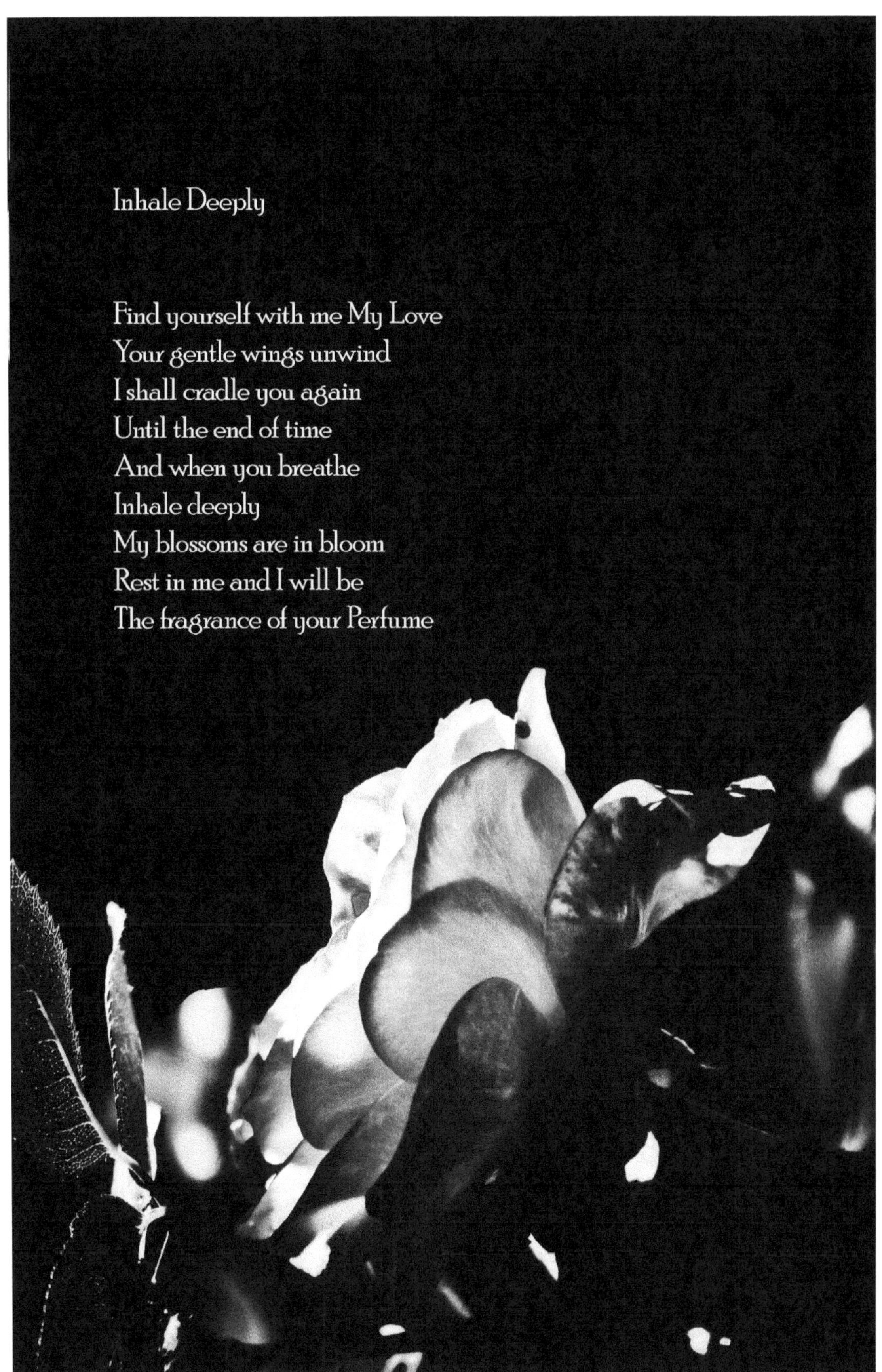

Inhale Deeply

Find yourself with me My Love
Your gentle wings unwind
I shall cradle you again
Until the end of time
And when you breathe
Inhale deeply
My blossoms are in bloom
Rest in me and I will be
The fragrance of your Perfume

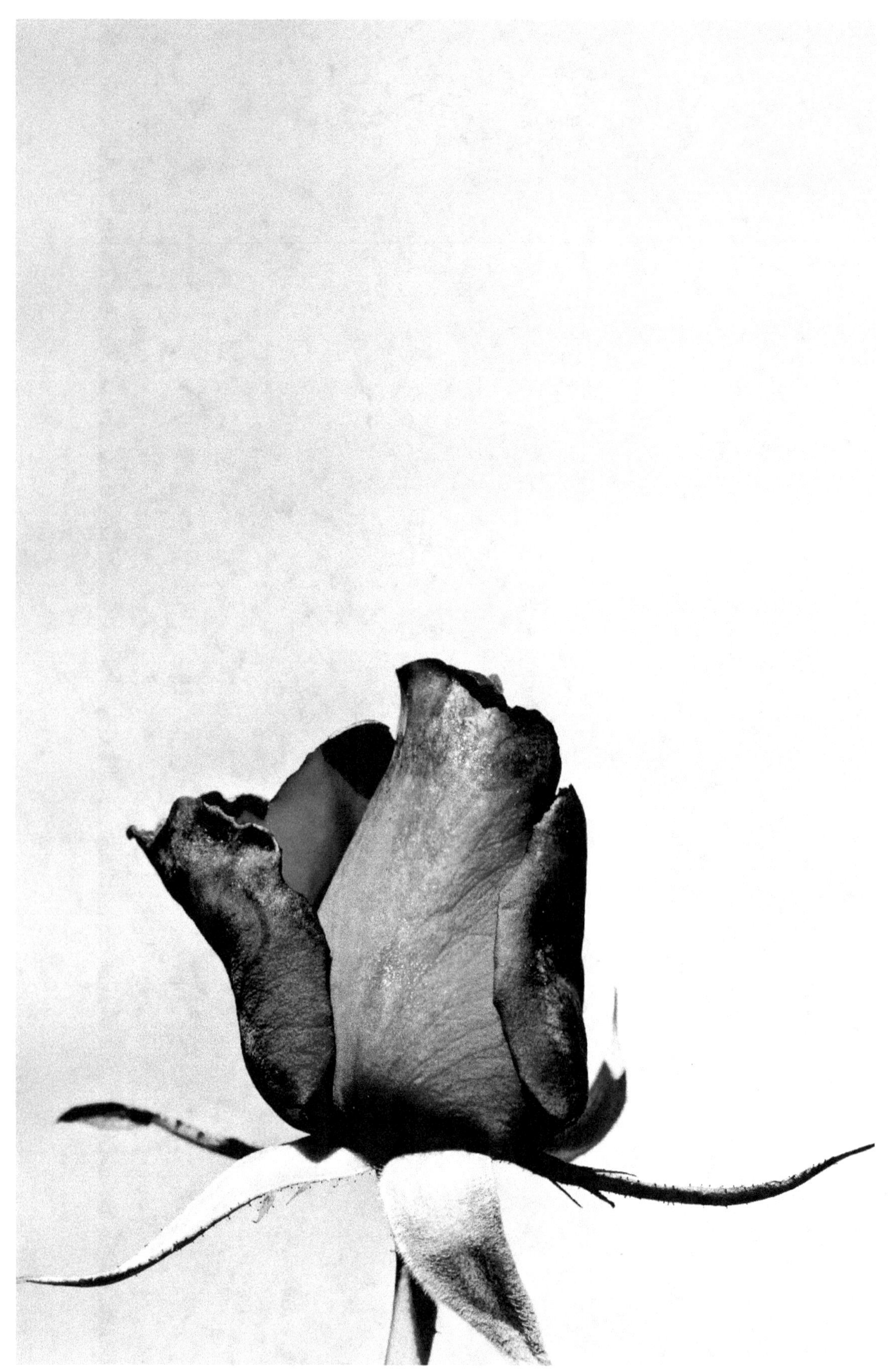

My Love Whispers

My Love you wear the rainbow
All colors touch your face
Even the gentle flowers say
From you they receive grace

My Love in all their glory
These flowers speak of you
Their beauty is your story
From your heart they all grew

They whisper Do I know you
I tell each flower this
My Love whispers I Love you
And seals it with a kiss

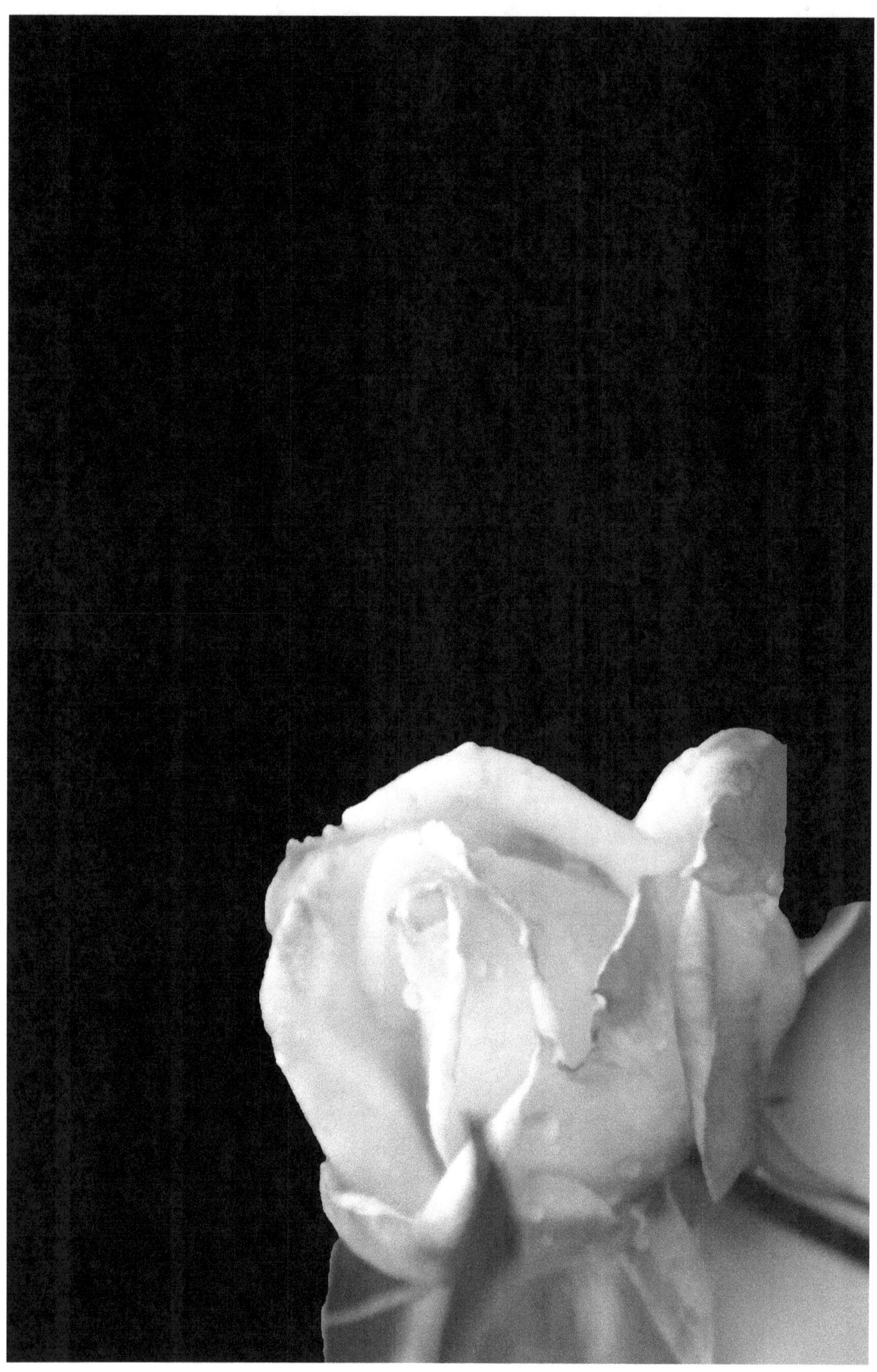

Dream Catcher

I have a dream - So it may seem
A dream of you - And I fall in Love
I fall in Love - No I run to you
Because it seems - You are my dreams
I make a wish - And say a prayer
I look up - And you are there
Your eyes are full - Your smile bright
Inside of you I see the light
You tell the truth - Love is your key
My life is bright - Because you see
I Love My Love - This you should know
Dear Dream Catcher - Let our Love grow

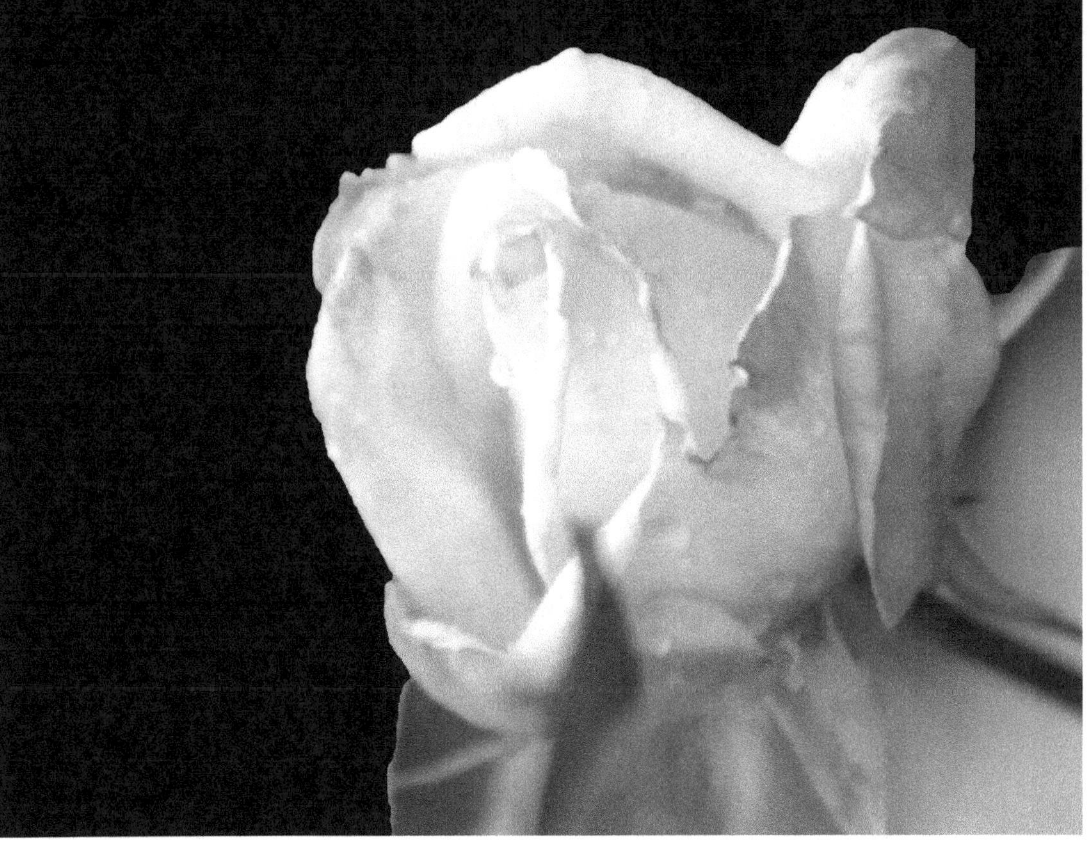

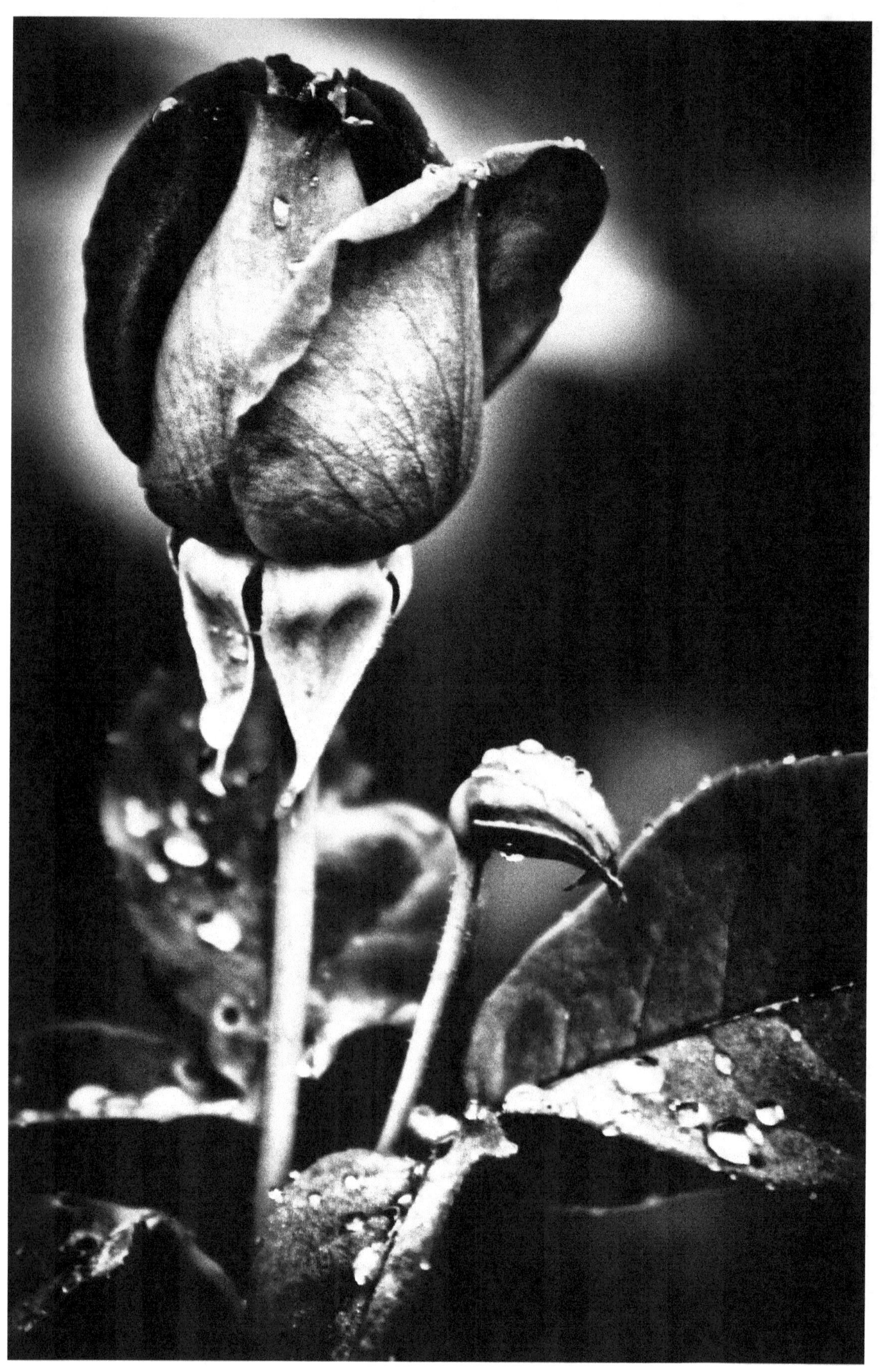

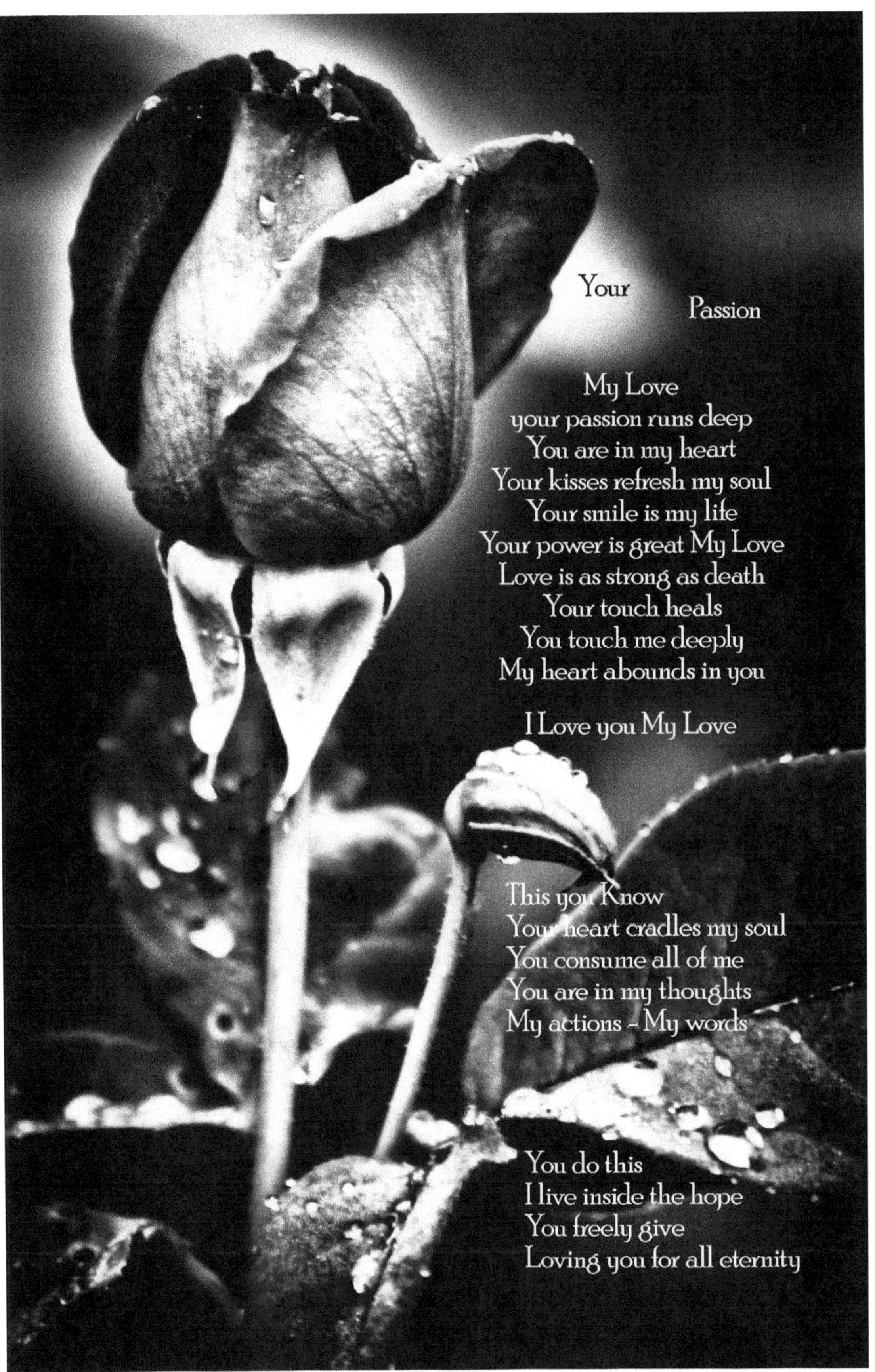
Your Passion
My Love
your passion runs deep
You are in my heart
Your kisses refresh my soul
Your smile is my life
Your power is great My Love
Love is as strong as death
Your touch heals
You touch me deeply
My heart abounds in you
I Love you My Love
This you Know
Your heart cradles my soul
You consume all of me
You are in my thoughts
My actions - My words
You do this
I live inside the hope
You freely give
Loving you for all eternity

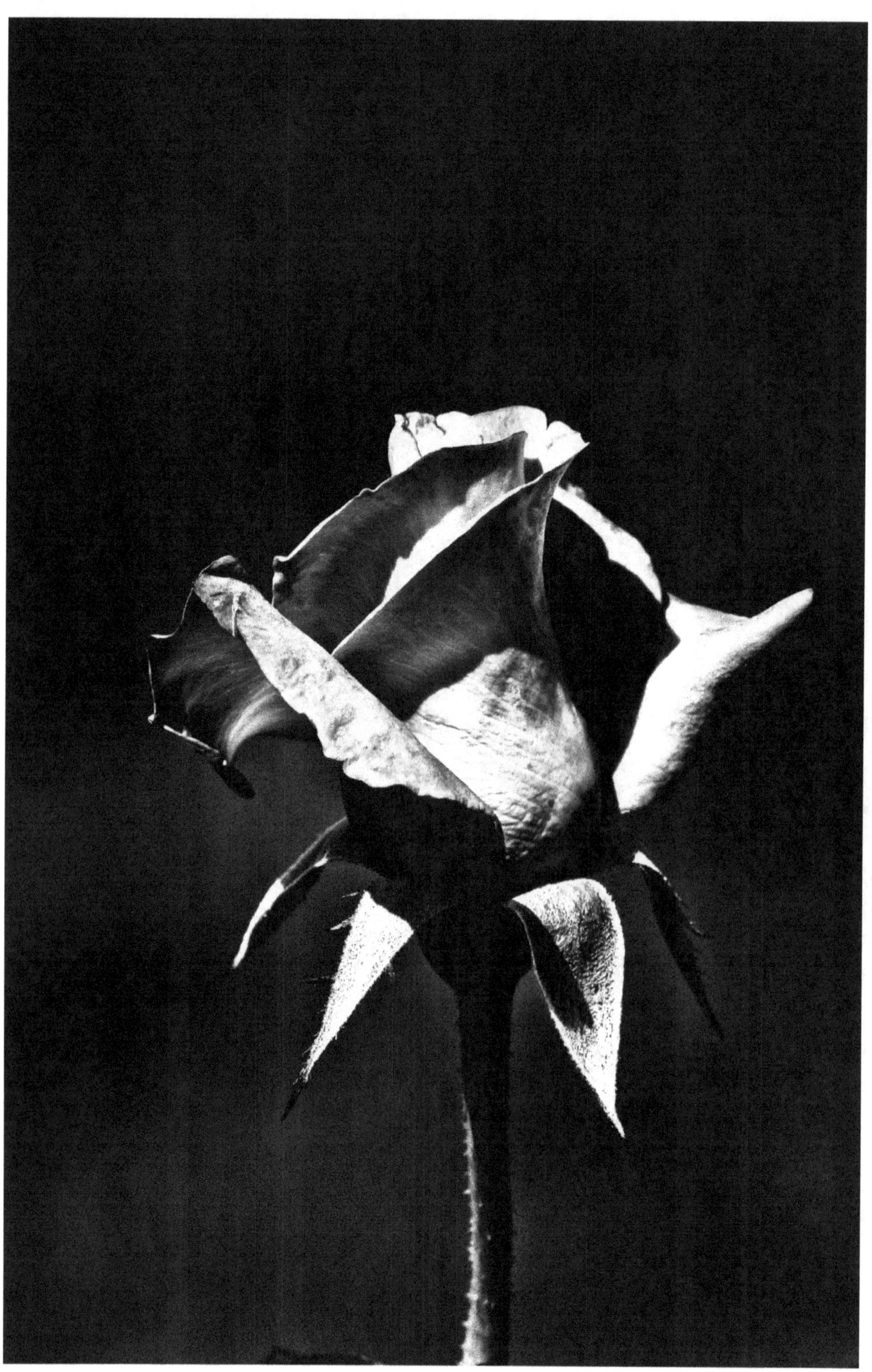

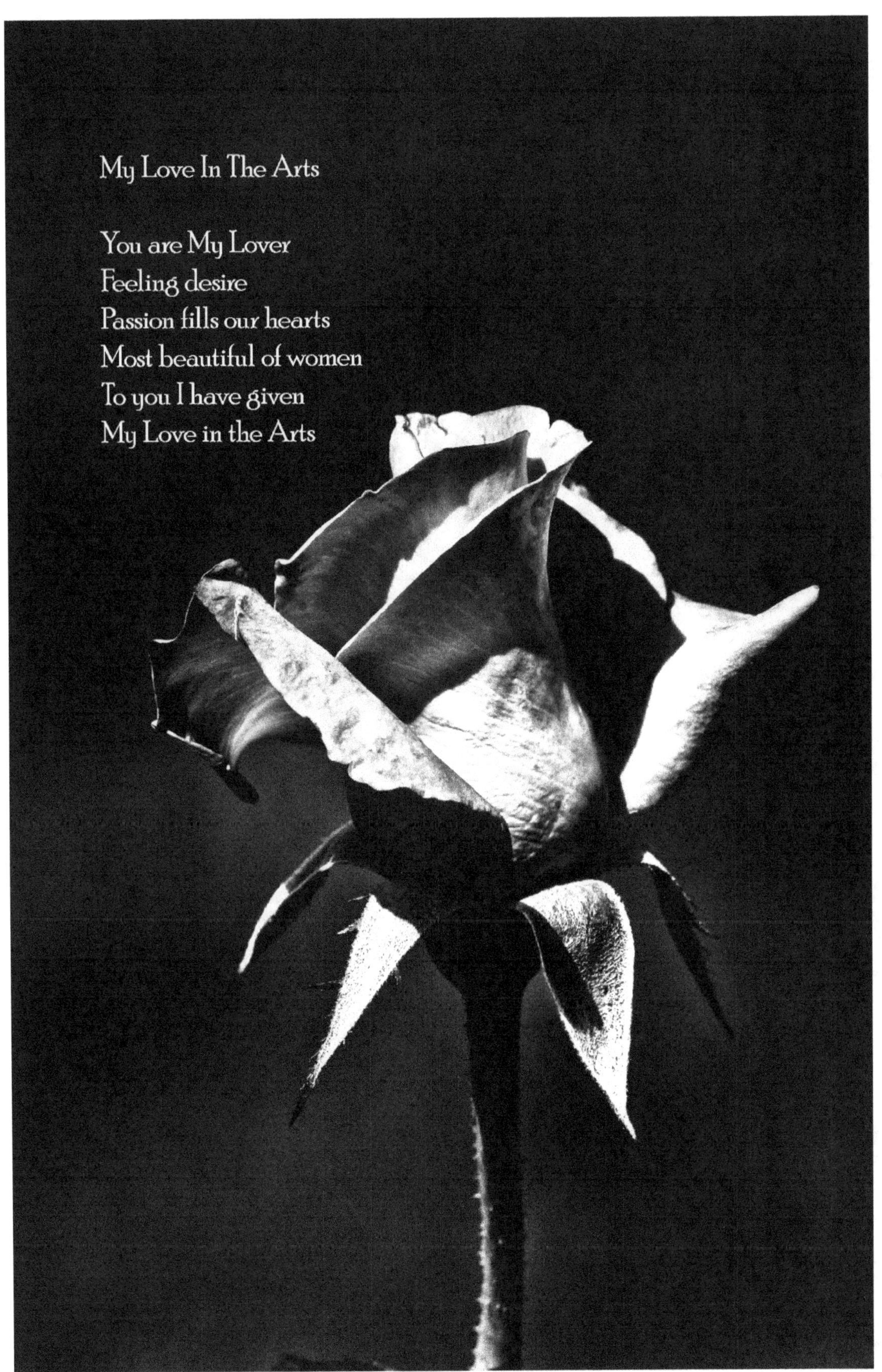
My Love In The Arts

You are My Lover
Feeling desire
Passion fills our hearts
Most beautiful of women
To you I have given
My Love in the Arts

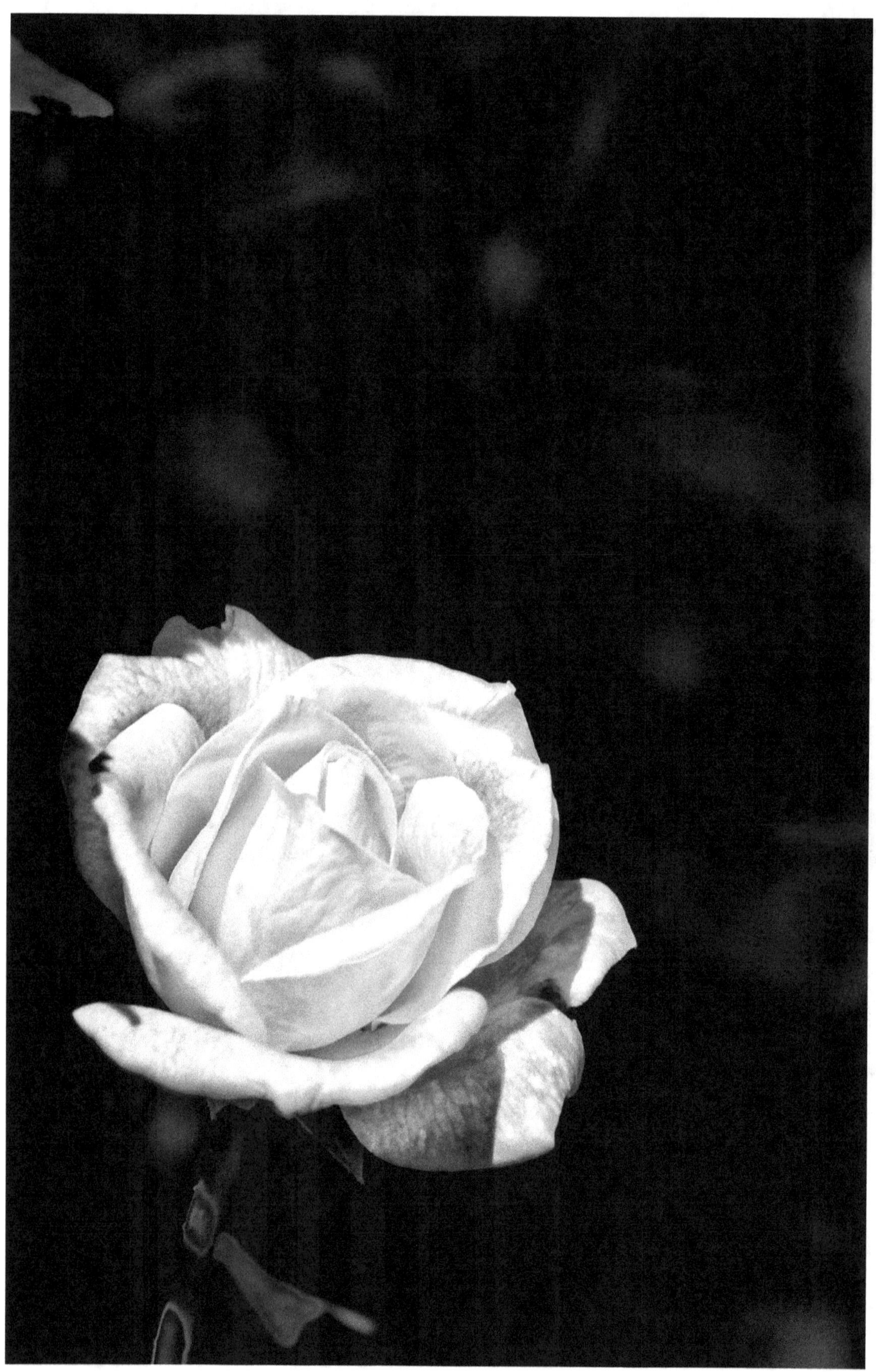

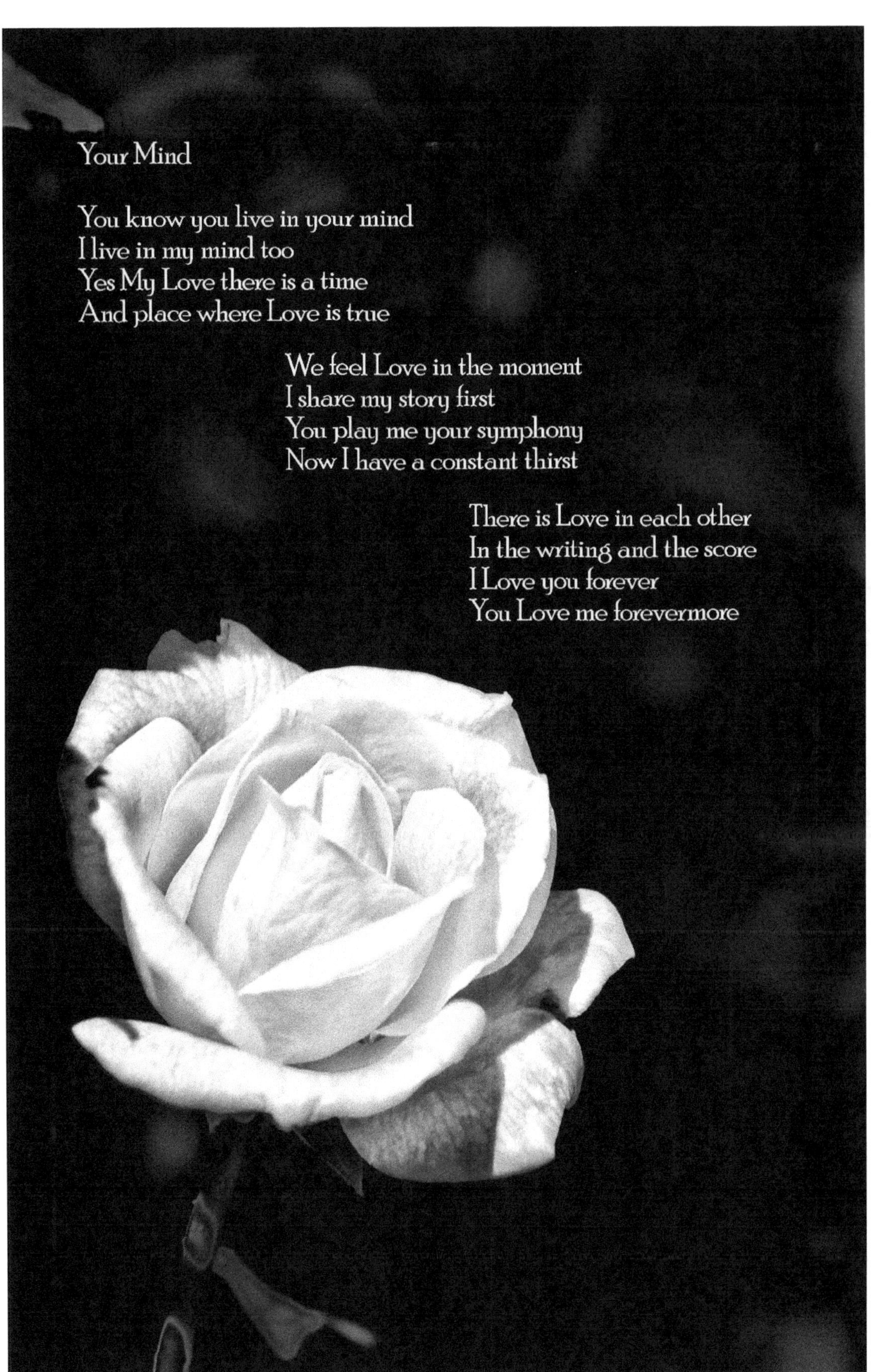

Your Mind

You know you live in your mind
I live in my mind too
Yes My Love there is a time
And place where Love is true

We feel Love in the moment
I share my story first
You play me your symphony
Now I have a constant thirst

There is Love in each other
In the writing and the score
I Love you forever
You Love me forevermore

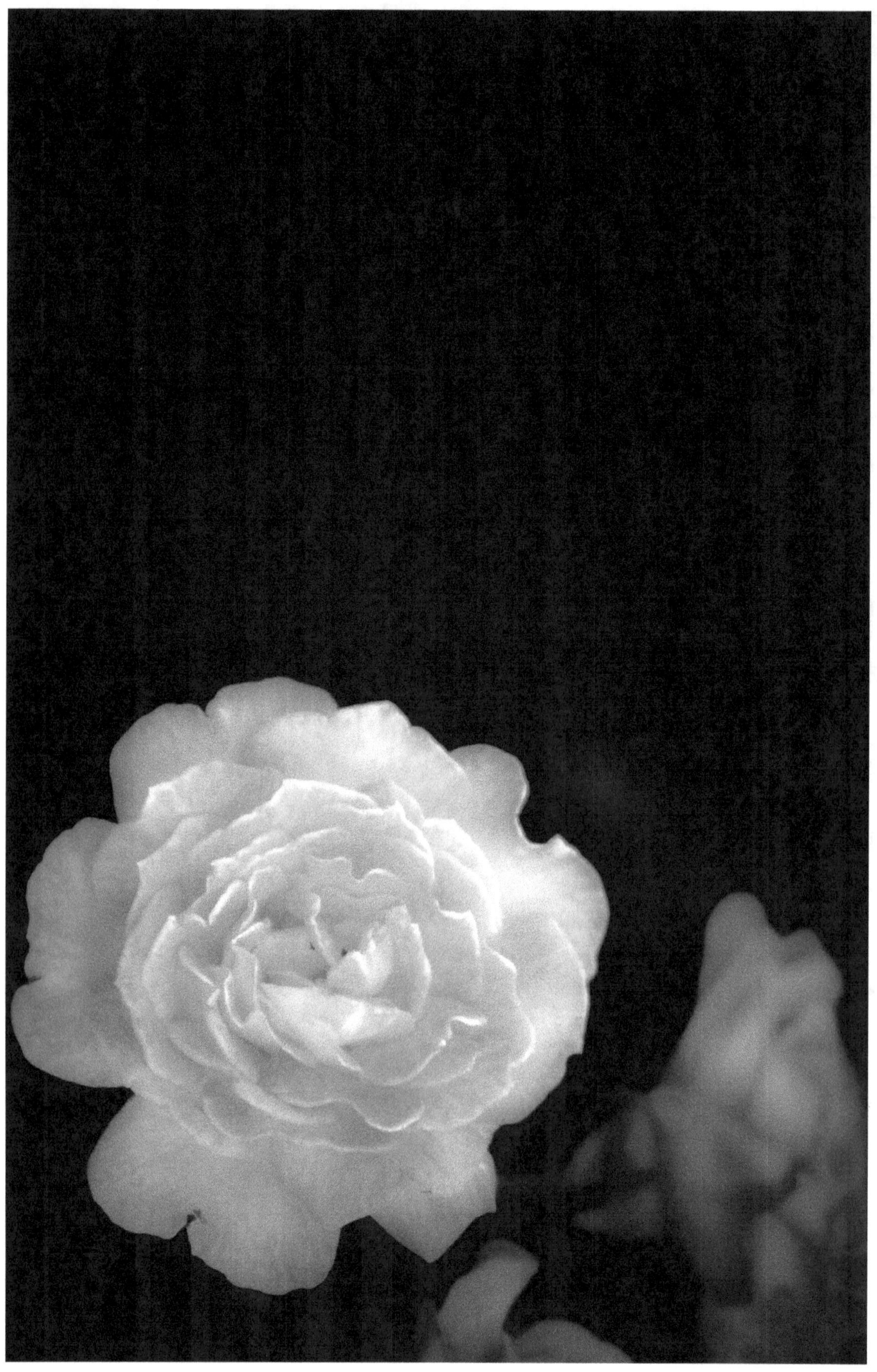

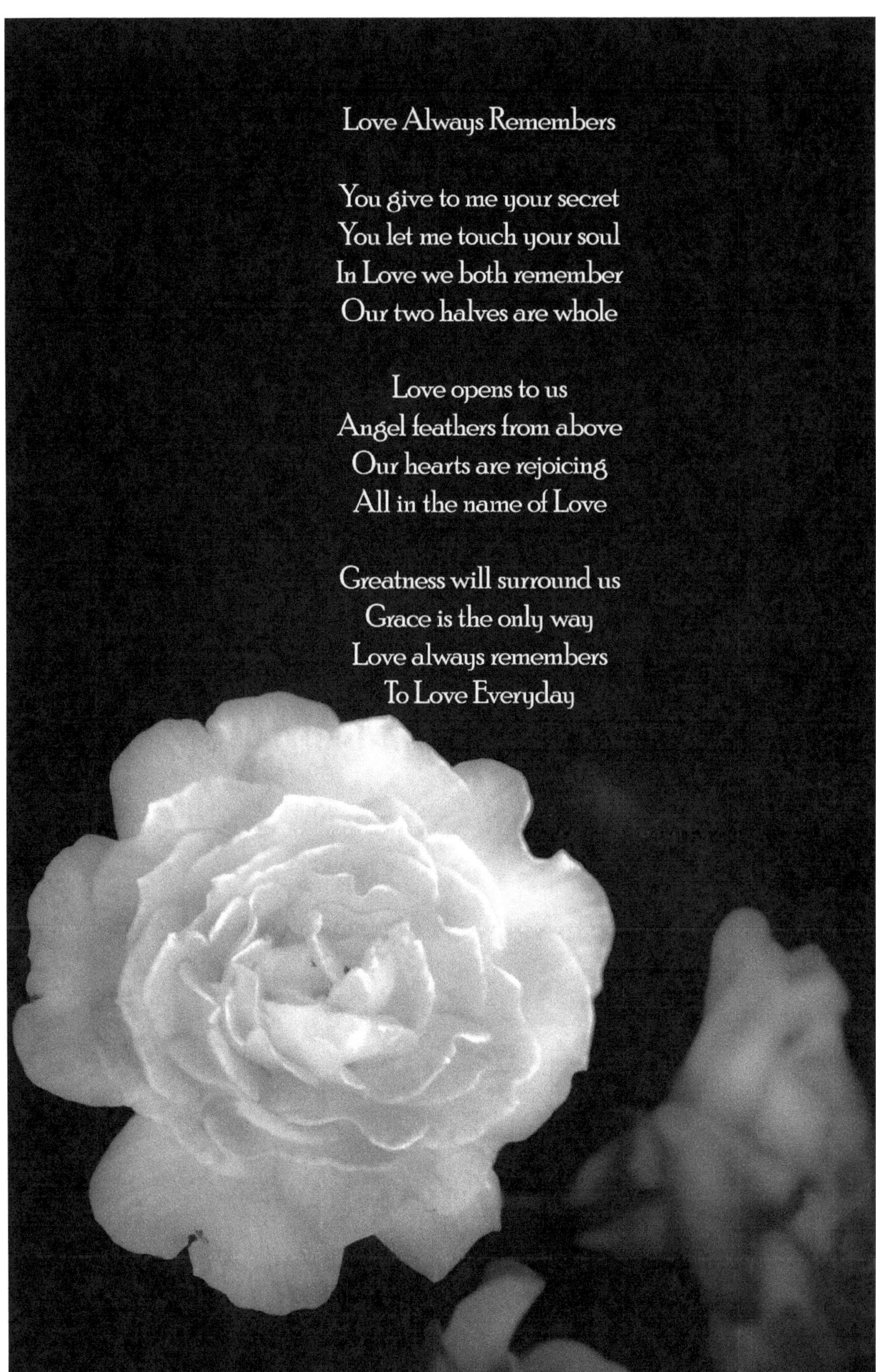

Love Always Remembers

You give to me your secret
You let me touch your soul
In Love we both remember
Our two halves are whole

Love opens to us
Angel feathers from above
Our hearts are rejoicing
All in the name of Love

Greatness will surround us
Grace is the only way
Love always remembers
To Love Everyday

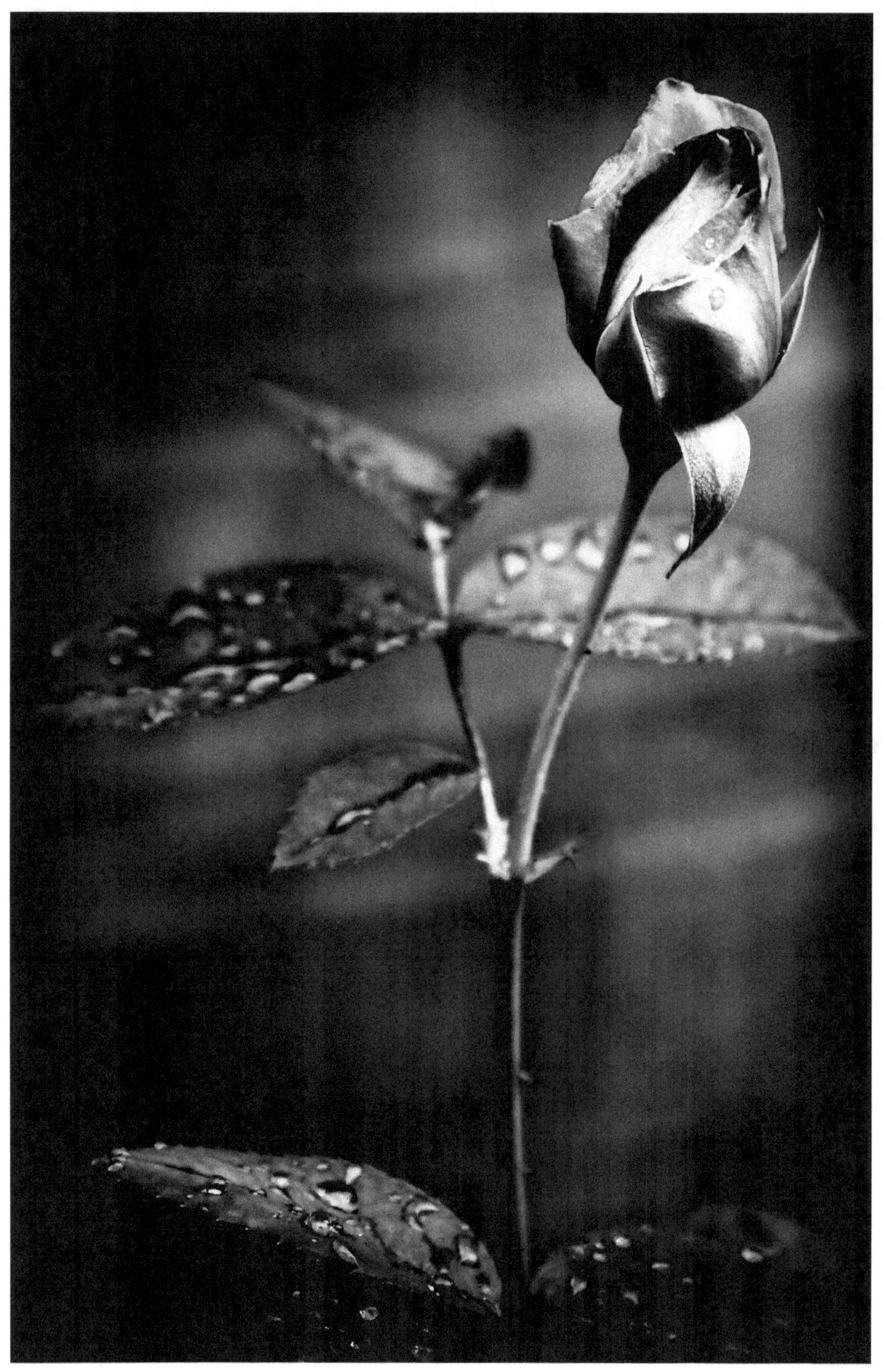

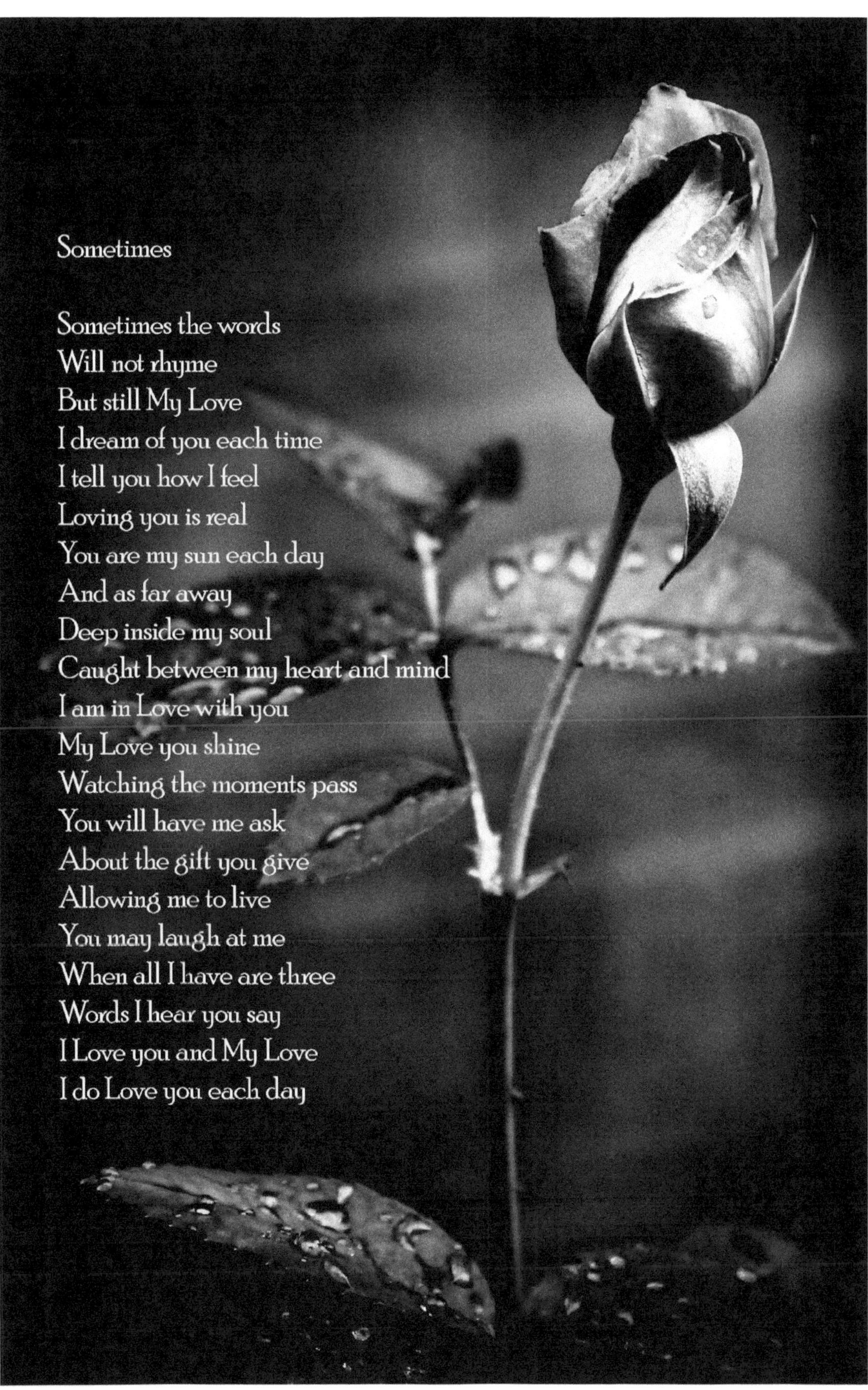

Sometimes

Sometimes the words
Will not rhyme
But still My Love
I dream of you each time
I tell you how I feel
Loving you is real
You are my sun each day
And as far away
Deep inside my soul
Caught between my heart and mind
I am in Love with you
My Love you shine
Watching the moments pass
You will have me ask
About the gift you give
Allowing me to live
You may laugh at me
When all I have are three
Words I hear you say
I Love you and My Love
I do Love you each day

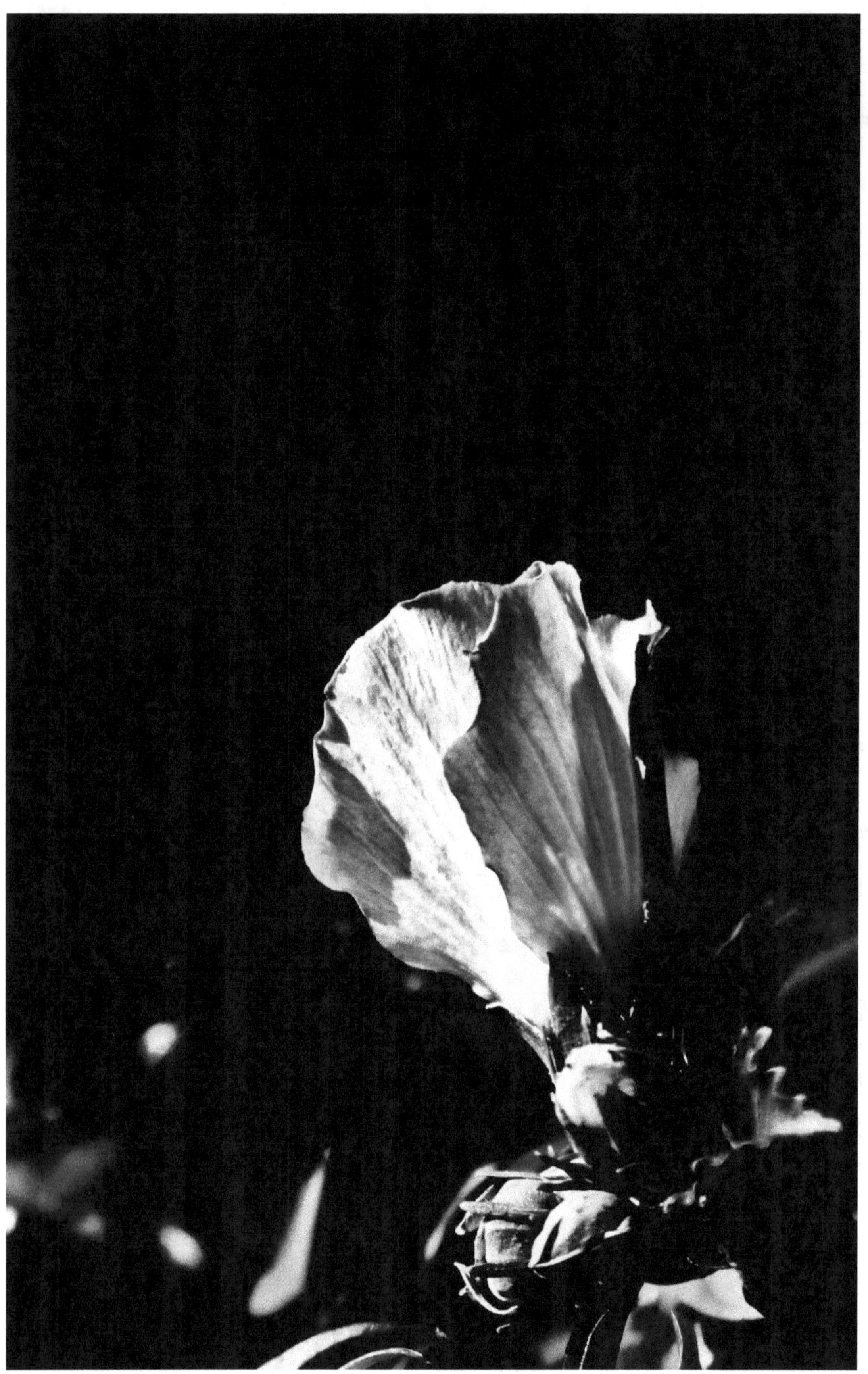

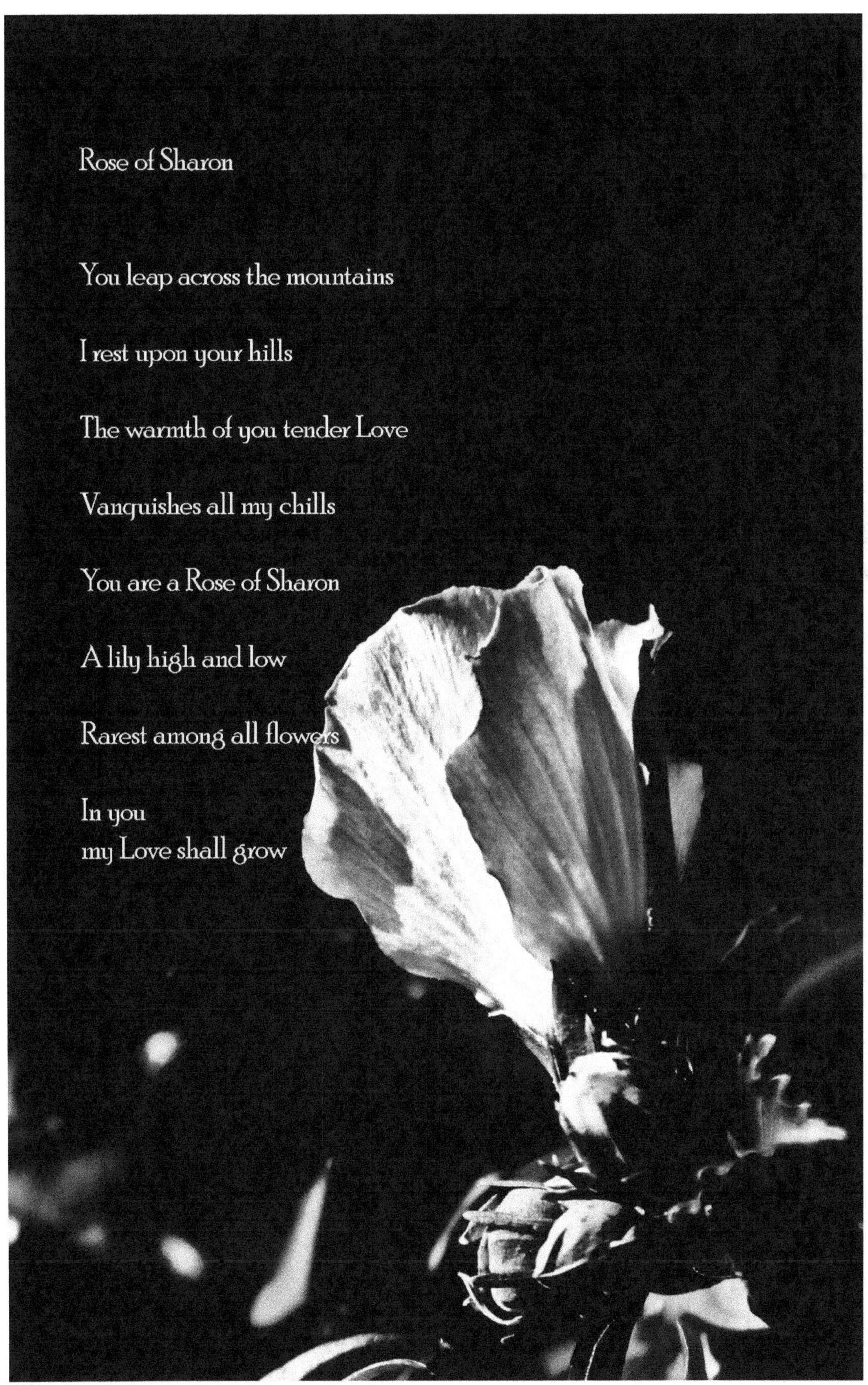

Rose of Sharon

You leap across the mountains

I rest upon your hills

The warmth of you tender Love

Vanquishes all my chills

You are a Rose of Sharon

A lily high and low

Rarest among all flowers

In you
my Love shall grow

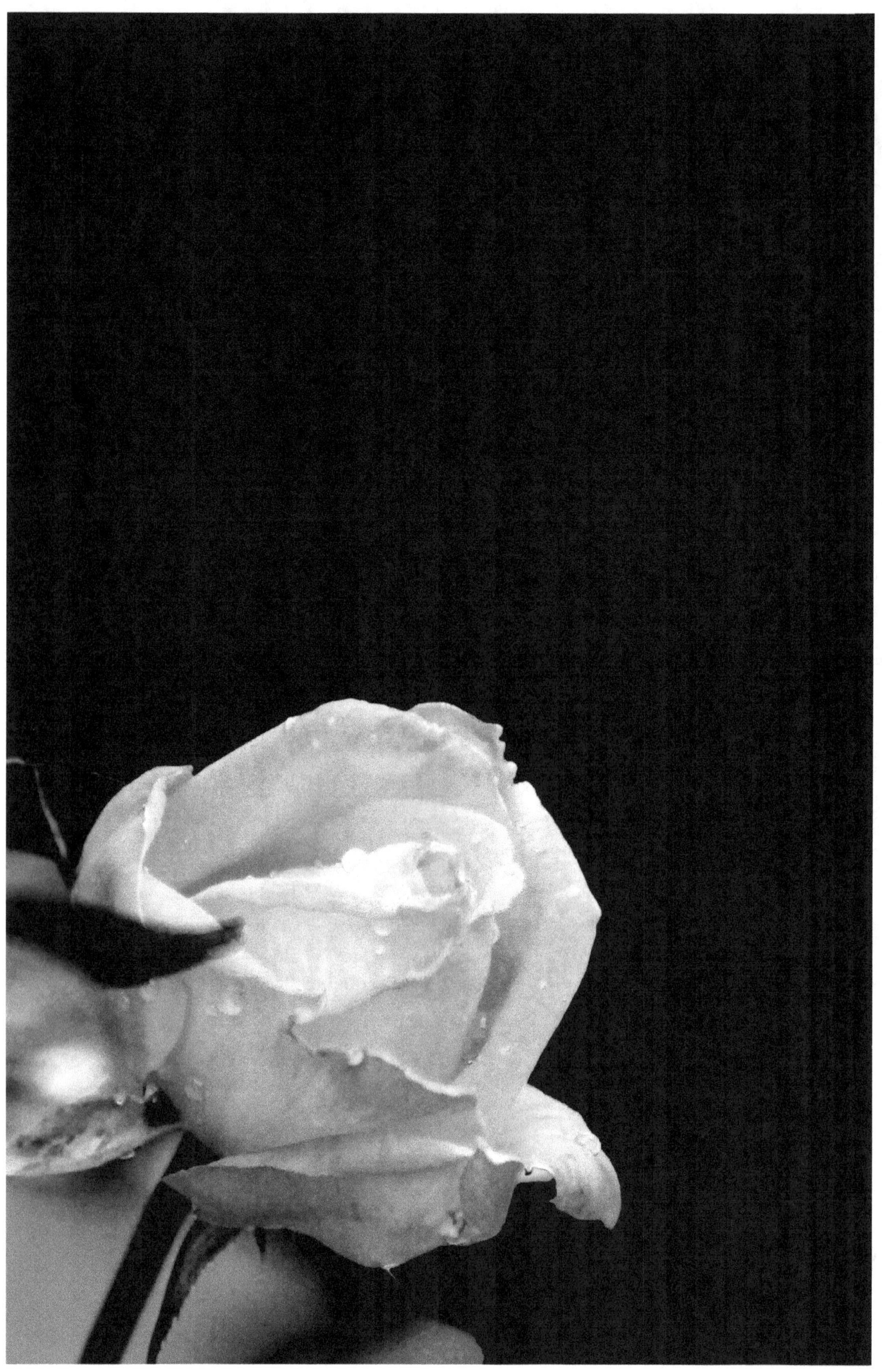

I Am In Love

With you I am In Love ~ My Love your mouth
Is sweetness itself ~ Your Lips are full
Like my desire for you

Your waist is ~ A mound of silk
Encircled by flowers ~ And creamy like milk

Your eyes are like pools ~ Refreshing and cool
Playground of your soul ~ Quenching my thirst

You are like the dawn ~ A majestic tapestry
Fairer than the moon ~ And brighter than the sun

I am In Love with you

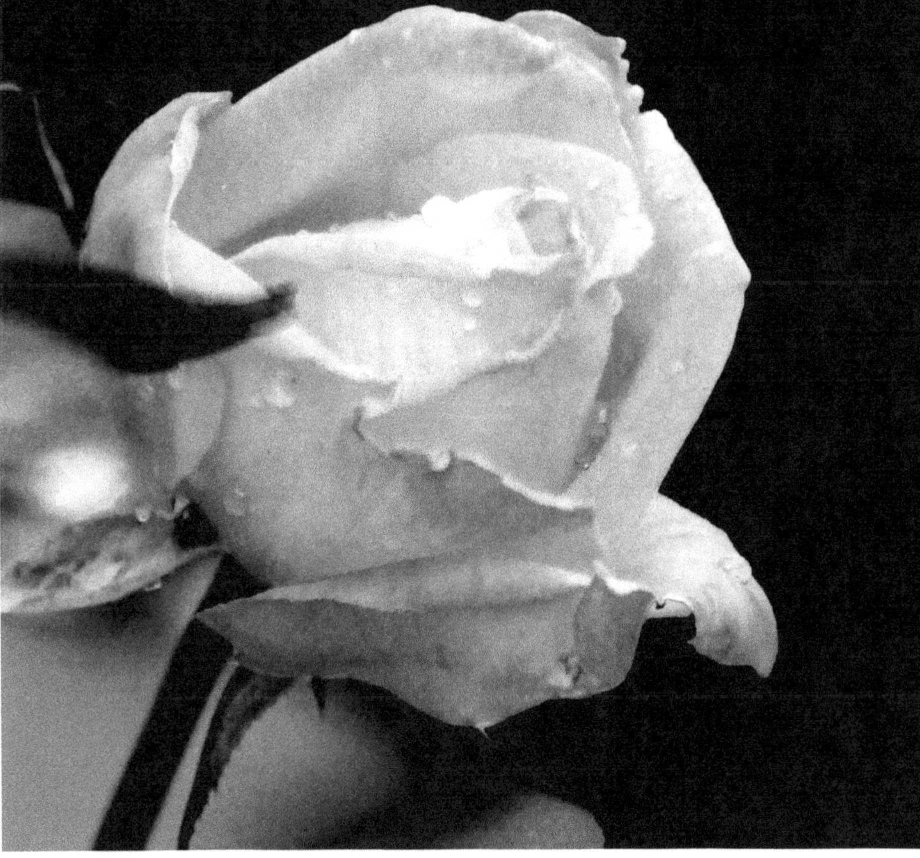

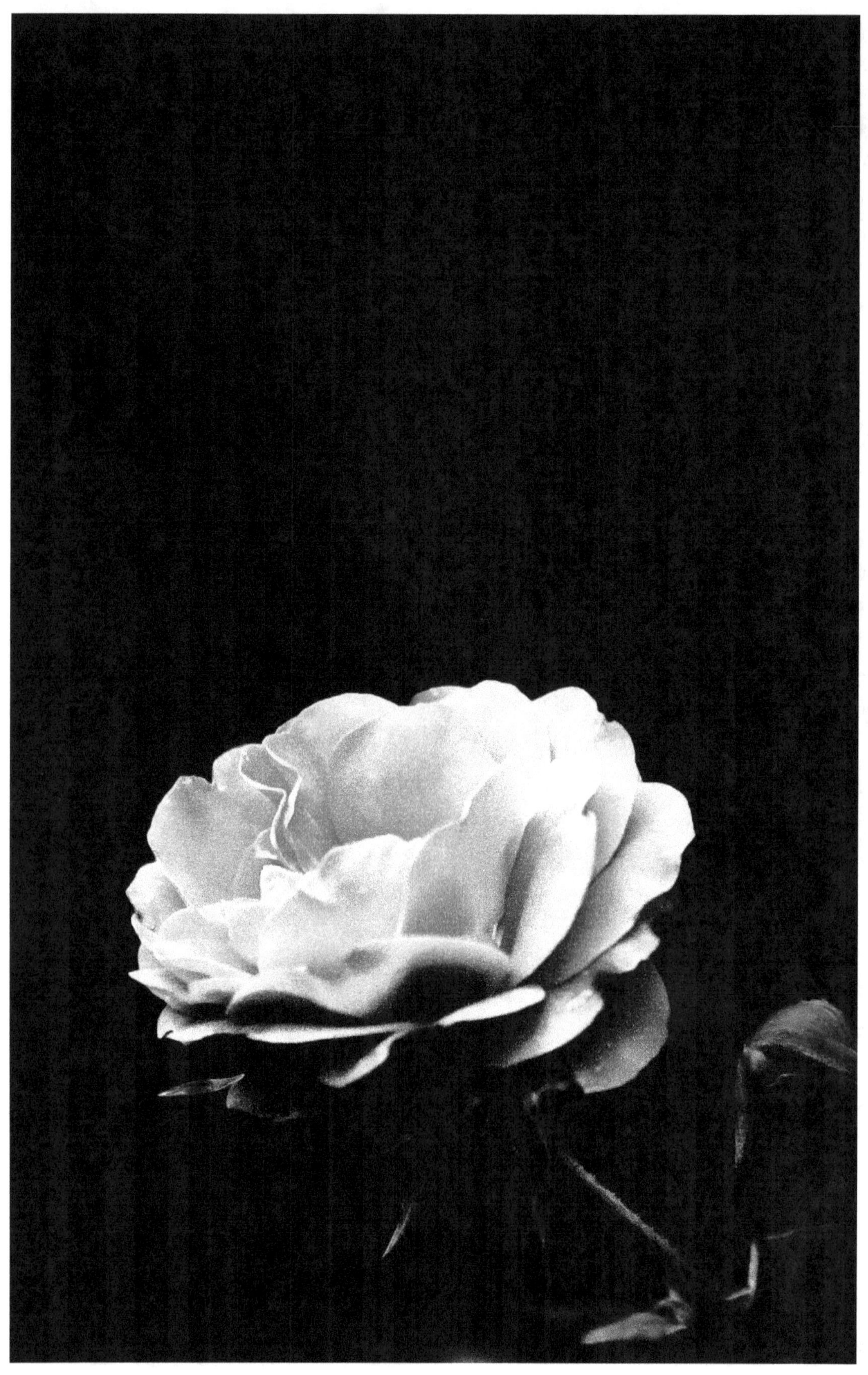

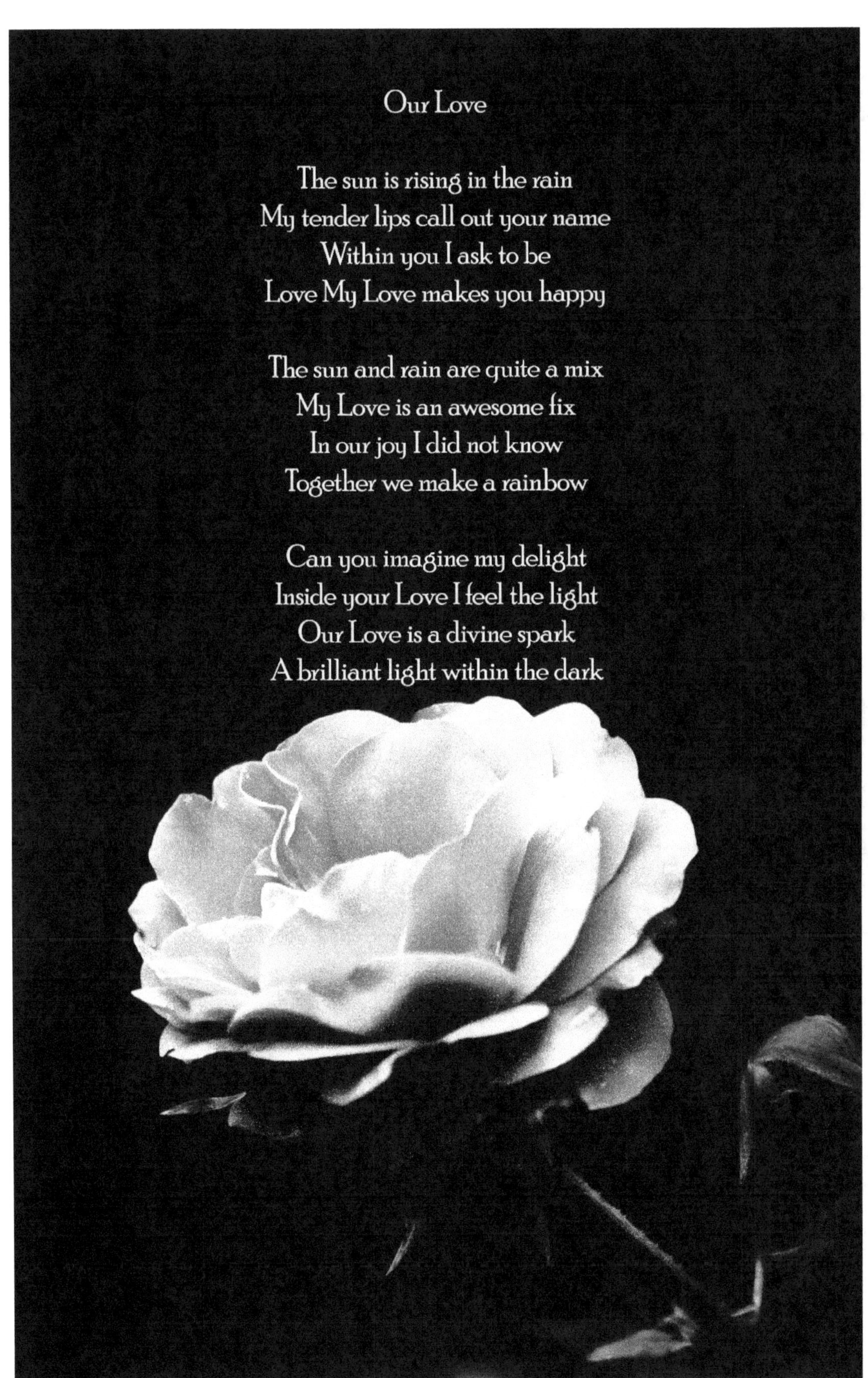
Our Love

The sun is rising in the rain
My tender lips call out your name
Within you I ask to be
Love My Love makes you happy

The sun and rain are quite a mix
My Love is an awesome fix
In our joy I did not know
Together we make a rainbow

Can you imagine my delight
Inside your Love I feel the light
Our Love is a divine spark
A brilliant light within the dark

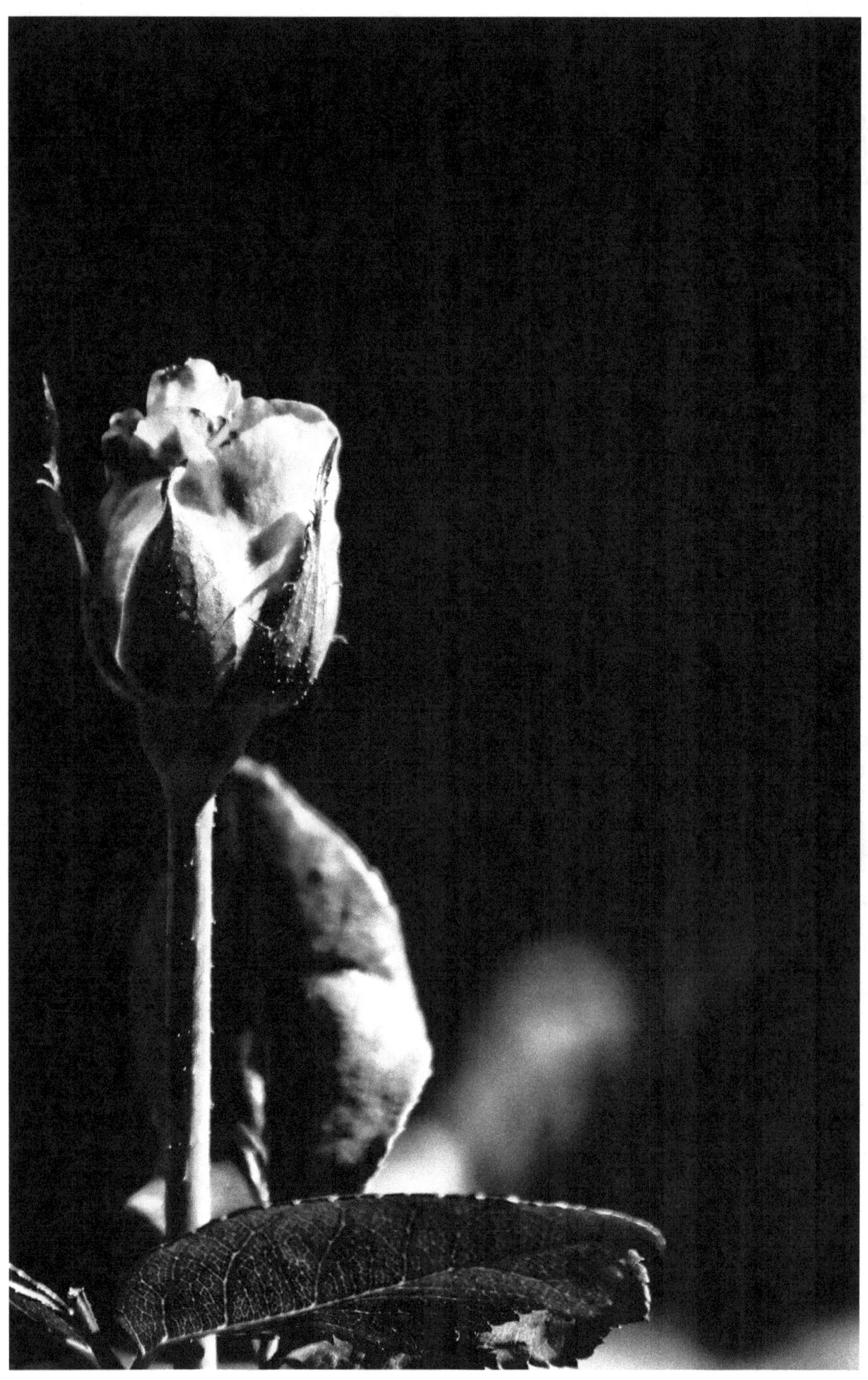

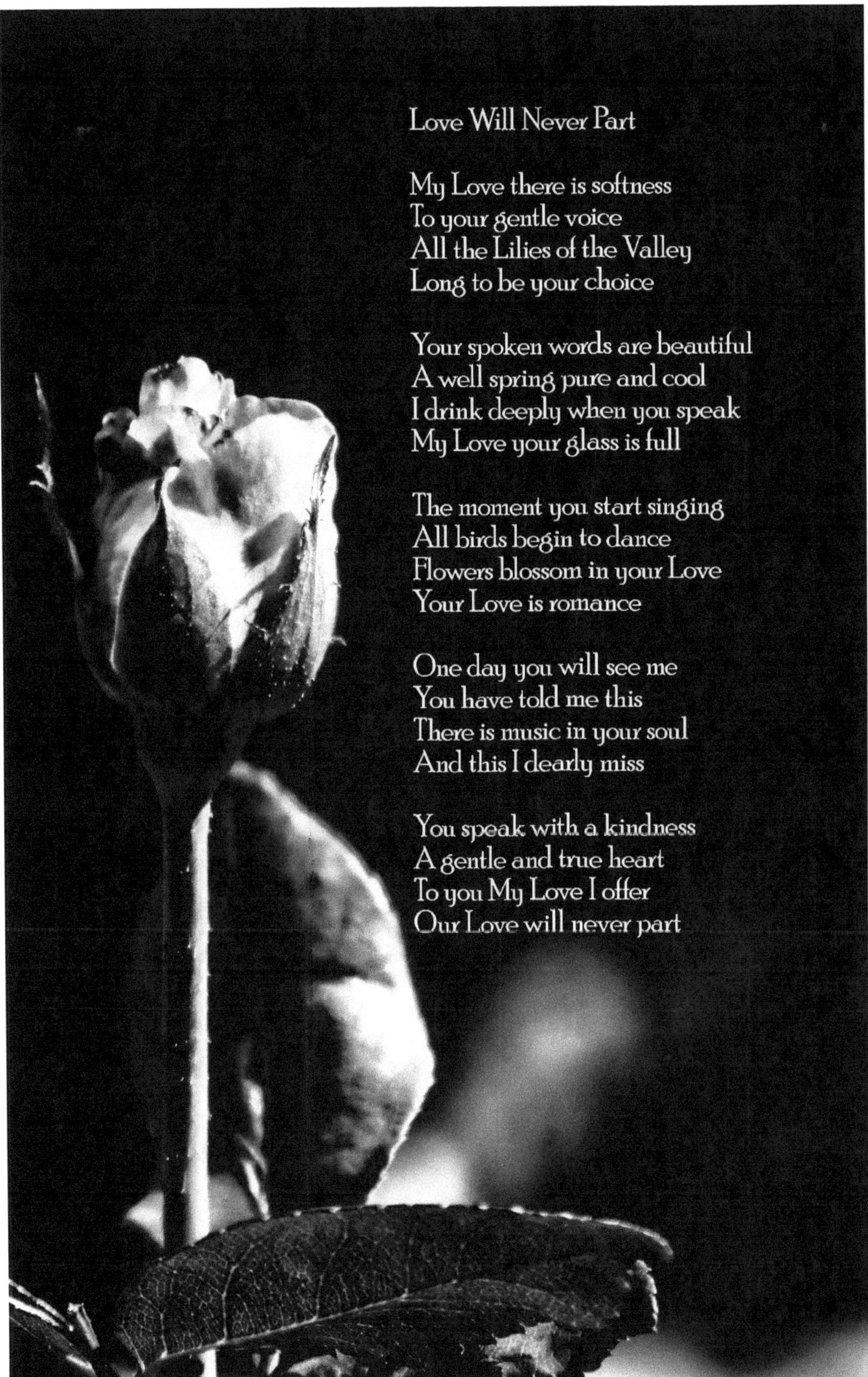

Love Will Never Part

My Love there is softness
To your gentle voice
All the Lilies of the Valley
Long to be your choice

Your spoken words are beautiful
A well spring pure and cool
I drink deeply when you speak
My Love your glass is full

The moment you start singing
All birds begin to dance
Flowers blossom in your Love
Your Love is romance

One day you will see me
You have told me this
There is music in your soul
And this I dearly miss

You speak with a kindness
A gentle and true heart
To you My Love I offer
Our Love will never part

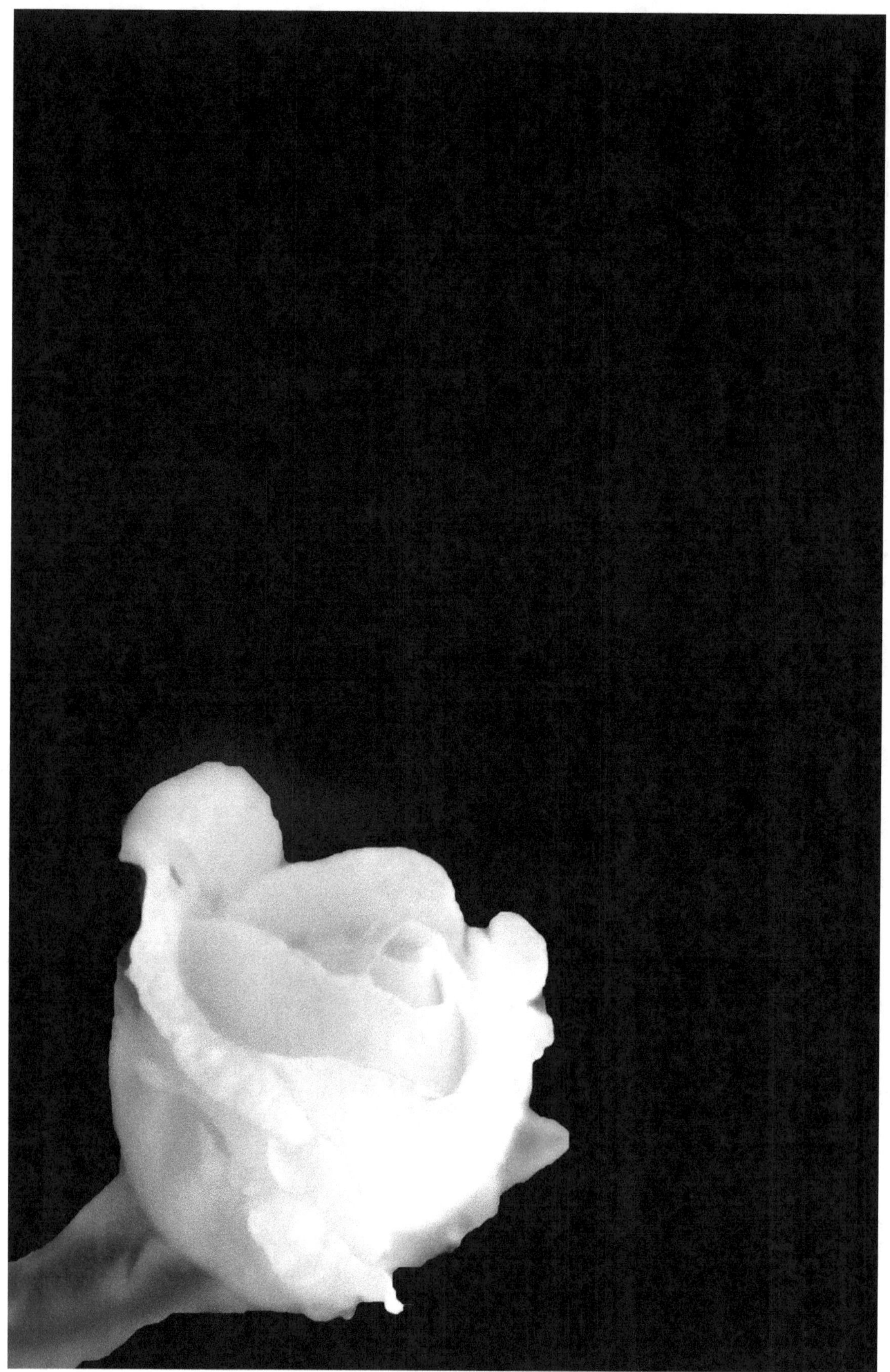

Live In Love Forever

Flowing like the rivers - My soul thirst for you
Supreme among all givers - I Love all you do

My Love you are an ocean - Pure and Cool and Sweet
I will drink you deeply - Every time we meet

My Love I lay in vineyards - My body longs for you
I can feel you cover me - Like lilies wet with dew

I gaze on your oasis - And touch eternity
My eyes are ever shining - You do this to me

There is life in your shelter - And Joy in your arms
I will slip into your pools - Lost in all your charms
Your eyes have a sparkle - Love is coming through
I'll live in Love forever - As long as I'm with you

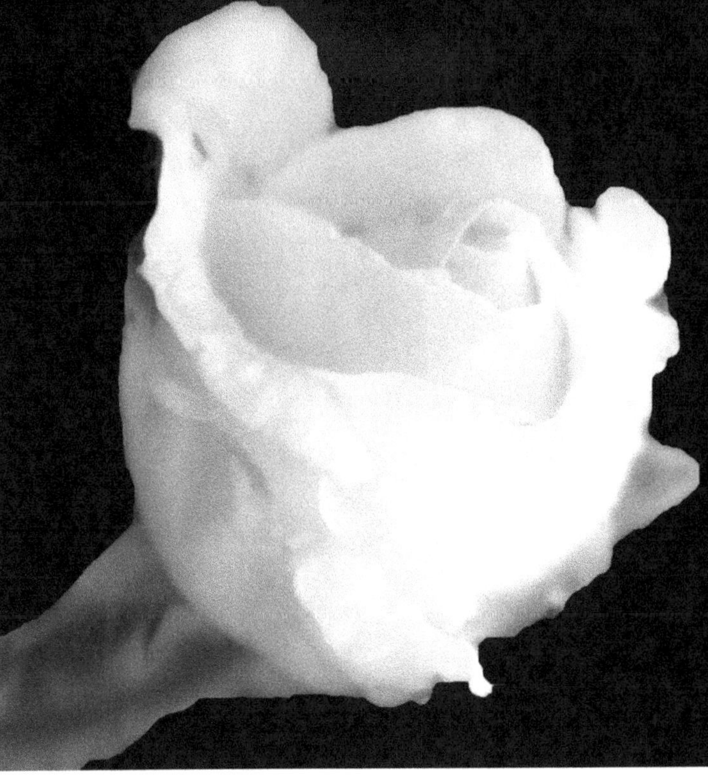

Dr. Claus combines his love of poetry, photography, and nature to create art.
His published works include:

A Gift of Love
A Hairy Scary Spider
Chuck Hug A Lunkle Ching Choo - Choo
Clair de Lune Serenade
Crumble Rumble Stumble Stew
Daughter Of Kings
Daughter Of Kings (Aquarelle)
Inhale Deeply
Inhale Deeply (Aquarelle)
Love Poems 101
Medley Mole Meets Buddy Rabbit
My Gentle Butterfly
My Love Whispers
My Love Whispers (Aquarelle)
My Love Whispers (Luz Celestial)
My Lover
My Lover (Aquarelle)
Parsifal
Poems
Poems Of Love
The Day And Night Before Christmas
The Keeper Of The Stones
The Light Of The Trees (El Corazon)
The Poetess
The Poetess (Aquarelle)
The Poetess (Luz Celestial)
The Promise
The Promise (Aquarelle)
The Promise (Luz Celestial)
To Thee I Sing
To Thee I Sing (Aquarelle)
To Thee I Sing (Luz Celestial)
When You Breathe
When You Breathe (Aquarelle)

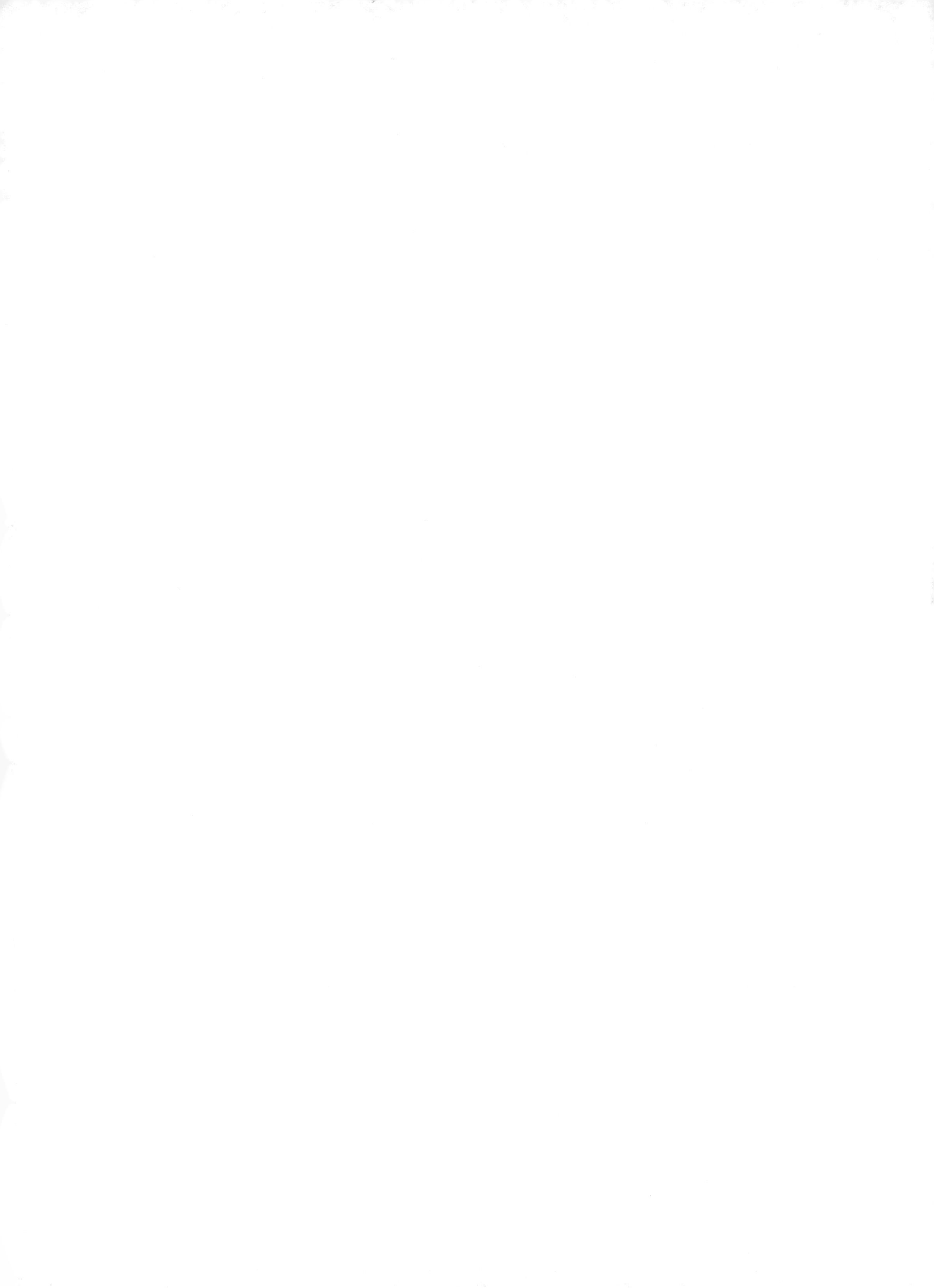

www.ingramcontent.com/pod-product-compliance
Lightning Source LLC
LaVergne TN
LVHW061253100826
845148LV00008B/1110

9781614970606